"In *From Stumbling Blocks to Stepping Stones,* Shari so poignantly describes the suffering she experienced as a learning-disabled child, yet her sense of humor and determination shine through. It jars the imagination to realize that a child deemed uneducable—even recommended for institutionalization—became a poised and gifted national lecturer with her master's degree in education! Shari is one of those rare people whose speaking and writing incites a lump in the throat one moment, then bursts of laughter and cheers the next, all for a child who beat incredible odds. Her insights about educational methods that helped and hindered her will impact teachers and offer great hope to struggling students and the parents who love and guide them."

—Laurie Winslow Sargent
Author of *Delight in Your Child's Design*

"Shari's story captures her charismatic style and personality in a humorous, engaging way. The reader is brought from laughter to tears as the agonies of Shari's struggle are described from the aspect of a child looking out through thick, horn-rimmed glasses. Every teacher who has attempted to teach students like Shari will find new ideas to reach them through the pages of this book. Every parent who has felt the pain of a child who could not sit still will be encouraged by Shari's mother's steadfast belief in her daughter. Those who struggle to learn will find that their difficulties are probably not as great as Shari's. Her power to overcome is a clear testimony of a faithful God who redeems all trials and turns them into stepping stones. Bravo, Shari. I salute you!"

—Dr. Kathleen R. Hopkins
Executive Director, National Institute
for Learning Development (NILD)

"Shari Rusch Furnstahl's book is filled with emotion and a sense of triumph. As I read it, I could feel the courage that Shari lived each day as she found a way to work through her adversity and help a positive solution surface in her life. Shari and her 'never give up' attitude will encourage and inspire anyone who reads this book.

"Readers will immediately identify with the author's main theme of love. But there is another true emotion Shari brings to this powerful testimony of triumph. Hope is there for anyone who can identify with the challenges Shari shares through her writing. As an Educational Administrator, I was excited by the hope Shari gives to youth or to those who know or have children who are challenged.

"In addition, the author's parenting solutions provide a fantastic guide for single parents, young parents, parents who need help in parenting, and parents who struggle with life as we all know it in today's world."

    —Bob Arkfeld
    Principal, Knowledge Quest Academy

"Our Father knit together the marvelous creation of Shari. Through her story, He will encourage and lighten the hearts of all who read it. If every educator, father, mother and student would read, *From Stumbling Blocks to Stepping Stones,* our schools would be stronger, happier, and safer for all children."

    —Louann Farnham
    Christian educator and director of an
    alternative multi-age school

From Stumbling Blocks *to*

Stepping Stones

Help and Hope for
Special Needs Kids

Tyndale House Publishers, Inc.
Carol Stream, Illinois

Shari Rusch Furnstahl M.Ed.

Editor: Liz Duckworth
Cover design: Joseph Sapulich
Cover photograph of girl © by Debi Bishop/istockphoto. All rights reserved.
Cover photograph of flower © by Marcin Paiko/istockphoto. All rights reserved.

Library of Congress Cataloging-in-Publication Data
Furnstahl, Shari Rusch, 1966-
  From stumbling blocks to stepping stones / Shari Rusch Furnstahl.
    p. cm.
  ISBN-13: 978-1-58997-435-7
  ISBN-10: 1-58997-435-2
  1. Furnstahl, Shari Rusch, 1966- 2. Learning disabled—Washington (State)—
Biography. 3. Parents of children with disabilities. I. Title.
  LC4705.5.W2F87 2007
  371.092—dc22
  [B]

                                                    2007010694

Printed in the United States of America
1 2 3 4 5 6 7 8 9 / 12 11 10 09 08 07

This book is dedicated to my family, my teachers,
and all those individuals who refused
to let my limitations have the last word

🐉

Acknowledgments

I wish to thank the following people for challenging me to reach my potential and reminding me that laughing is better than crying any day.

My sister, Shawn, for being a role model, my mom for giving brownies to people who didn't like me, and my dad for pretending I was normal.

Michael, the second boy I fell in love with. You remind me that differences are beautiful and that nothing is impossible.

Jessica, you have taught me that everything can be seen as a treasure and that even a princess can be a good soccer player.

Kelly and Chloe, you have taught me to never turn my back, to be concerned when it gets too quiet, and that window cleaner will remove Sharpie marker from most household surfaces. Oh, and that good things come in pairs!

Dave, the person who handed me a laptop and said, "Write." Thank you for always believing in me.

To every teacher, principal, maintenance worker, classified staff member, or paraprofessional who ever befriended me, thanks for giving me Kleenex to wipe my nose, someone to sit next to at lunch or hang out with at recess, for filling my toolbox full of strategies, and most of all—thanks for giving me hope for the future.

Most of all, thank You, God, for transforming my stumbling blocks into stepping stones.

Contents

Introduction

When I found out I was pregnant, I was really excited—for about five minutes. Then I began to worry. I had always been pretty good at worrying, but somehow this whole "mom thing" caused me to become—dare I say—irrational. Will I be a good mother? What college will my child go to? Will I be able to afford to send my child to college? And so on and so on. In the middle of the night I would wake up in a cold sweat worrying about recent studies cited on the evening news concerning red dye in candy, nitrates in hot dogs, hormones in milk, and the supposed danger in metal fillings. I think you get the idea.

After six years of marriage my husband was probably relieved that his diet soda habit and my belief it caused dementia were no longer the center of attention, but he tried to understand my concerns as I shed tears about the ozone layer and how it might affect the future of our unborn child. He would gently remind me that everything is in God's hands.

I knew he was right. I am a person of faith, so this whole worrying thing just doesn't make sense. I should trust God. Absolutely. So where did all this worry come from? I hate to make excuses, but I can honestly say that my growing up years were a hit parade of Murphy's Laws. "When you least expect it, expect it" became my motto. Though I came to know God early, I tended to keep Him in my hip pocket and rely on my own strength when the going got rough. I thought if I anticipated bad things, I would be ahead of disappointment. Sadly, I used prayer as a co-conspirator in my worry. Instead of completely trusting the God who made the universe to handle whatever was going on in my life, I would cover everything under the sun with prayer. I'd name every specific issue in the world and then worry I had left something out. Are you getting obsessive yet?

Oddly enough, I had somehow managed to reach levels of success even while being predisposed to anticipating the worst. Clearly God had His hand on me.

As soon as I learned I was pregnant, I applied the same "worst-case scenario" approach to our unborn child: praying against every single disability known to man, including learning disabilities, vision problems, motor coordination problems, club foot, and various environmental issues such as an overprotective mother who worries too much.

When Michael was born, we didn't hear, "It's a boy"; we heard, "We have a cleft problem here." I wondered how, if I had sufficiently worried (and prayed, but emphasis on the worry) throughout my whole pregnancy, I had not anticipated this.

I hadn't even held him yet, and we were already hearing about speech, hearing, dental, and other problems that could result from this "birth defect" (cleft lip and sub-mucous cleft palate). We were told that he would need at least three major surgeries, as well as extensive orthodontia. I was terrified.

Then I saw him. His eyes were beautiful. He had lovely long fingers and toes and was very alert. His lip and nose, well, they looked a little different. Really different. His face below his nose was open.

I had just been ushered into a new phase of my life. I was a mom and my child had "special needs." I wanted to be optimistic, but I had my own life experiences to back up my anxiety about Michael's future. I could recall such painful memories, remembering the names I was called and the alienation I felt because I was so different.

I could already feel myself slipping into something I had hoped I would never do: I was about to begin to hold my son back. Even in those first moments of life I was starting to transfer my feelings about life onto Michael. How unfair!

When Michael went down the hall for his first checkup, I had a really good talk with myself. There was some serious crying involved, and I think some sobbing occurred. I allowed my shoulders to slump and my head to rest in my hands. I already knew I wasn't going to be a perfect mother. The only thing I knew for sure was I wanted Michael to gain confidence about God and not learn to fear the world. As I had often reminded myself, *Thankfully, I know God.*

Oh, and thankfully, I married Dave. He is the normal half of this couple. Aside from a few bullies he encountered on his way to parochial school, he managed to come away from his childhood relatively unscathed. I knew he would be my balance. Every time I "over worried" about Michael, I knew Dave would help me get perspective and remind me to trust in God.

Though I still worried about mad cow disease and earthquakes, in the days and weeks to come I had many opportunities to shed layers of my own insecurities and childhood experiences through Michael. Every time someone looked at Michael and gasped, I had to take a deep breath and be willing to not allow someone else's response to shape our movement in the world. In the end, we still had to go to the grocery store.

After his first surgery there were plenty of negative assessments projected about Michael's future from well-meaning physicians, and from time to time we heard unthinking comments from strangers. In these situations I would remind myself that God is a miracle worker. I had to focus not on what a test or individual said, but on the bigger picture: The Lord was powerful enough to take the scar on Michael's face and any physical or emotional barriers caused by it and turn them into strength that Michael could use to fulfill his purpose in life.

On days when I was particularly caught up in concern for Michael, I would reflect on a thick file that followed me throughout my education. It was filled with worst-case scenarios and negative outcomes. The assessments and predictions in the file were probably accurate, but nothing in my file took into account the wonderful people who would help me and the other blessings only God could have sent. Remembering people who helped me and staying focused on that help gave me much hope for Michael.

With help I did reach far beyond assessments and labels to find success in areas such as speaking, writing, and teaching— success many people would have deemed impossible. That is really the essence of my story: Anyone can succeed with support and sometimes alternative methods to achieve success.

Nothing can prepare a parent or caregiver for special issues such as birth defects, learning disabilities, and other hidden and not-so-hidden handicaps, but we need to know, believe, and affirm that—just like me—Michael (and every other child for that matter), can achieve his potential regardless of a negative outcome predicted by a standardized test or medical assessment. Even if there are real physical, learning, or emotional challenges, it is important to realize that most limits are projected onto us. Sadly, if we hear enough about limits, in time we begin to believe in them.

While my inclination, and maybe yours, is to envision worst-case scenarios, we really don't have time for them. All children can succeed, but they need our love, our support, and most of all, our belief that they are more than the sum of their disabilities. We need to envision their success and help them see it too.

With personal experiences still fresh in my memory, I could view life and other people through a narrow prism of diminished potential and disabilities. My faith in God has enabled me to rise above this "deficit model" and strive to be a parent and teacher who believes in the greatness of a child even when he or she is running around the room for no apparent reason or is unintelligible when speaking. Not long ago, that was me. I can see that with effective strategies and methods, even a child who can't pay attention long enough to write his or her name can eventually write an essay.

Experiences as an LD (learning disabled) child have made me want to give nothing but my best as a teacher. I set the bar high and pray that any special child with whom I have contact will progress beyond any lesser assessments made about him or her. As a parent of four children, even with all my limitations, and even while worrying about pesticides and their potential to cause cancer, I have learned to have high expectations, draw upon strengths in my children, and act as their advocate. Above all, in every role I hold, I pray that God will direct and guide my path, giving me wisdom.

If you are a parent reading this book and you are discouraged, please take heart. Kids can overcome, go around, and go under the challenges before them. It does take intervention and strategies to make progress, and the path each child takes may be different from what we expected. Hopefully, we can change our mind-sets and view kids not through our measure of success or past failures, but through their best efforts at the time. God doesn't make mistakes. The precious children we are given, while challenged in whatever way, have a purpose and a mission. It is up to us—with help in this endeavor—to find that purpose and mission.

If you are a teacher and wondering how in the world you will ever stay in the profession because it is taxing emotionally and physically, hold on. Focus less on predictions and more on what you can do today to make a difference in that certain child's life. Make personal connections with students and continue to search for new strategies that will make a difference. Above all, keep praying that whatever you can't provide, God will.

If you are a student reading this book, and you have learning issues or other special needs, I have a message for you. You can achieve almost anything that you want to in life. So many of the things that still challenge me—writing, reading, and in some cases speaking—are now the very things at which I make a living. I stare at a blank page knowing in advance that I will get much of the spelling wrong, that my grammar will be less than perfect (an understatement), and that some words will be written backward or omitted. The good news is that it does get better. The more you hone your skills and develop your strategies, the easier it will become. I keep facing that blank page, using technical aides such as spell check and depending on other people for support, so what I write will make sense on paper.

I can't do anything alone. I often need audio books to help with reading or have someone read out loud what I need to learn through the written word. In almost every way, I have to ask for help. You might need to ask for help too, but there is no shame in that. Just think of it as moving one step closer to your dreams and goals.

What truly makes even the most difficult experience bearable is faith that God has an intention for my life. He gave me strengths, and I am able to see those now amid and beyond the challenges with which I was born. I have a purpose, and I cling to it knowing I was intended for greatness and a higher calling. This is what enables me to get up in front of a room filled with administrators and teachers and speak, when I know full well I was a child with a speech impediment. Raise your expectations for yourself high, even if no one else does, and believe you can and will achieve a great purpose in life.

I pray whoever reads this book will be inspired knowing that

God can use even the least of these to make a difference in the world; that our limitations are not larger than His plan for our lives.

God can use even the least of these to make a difference in the world; that our limitations are not larger than His plan for our lives.

This book is divided into two sections. First is my story—all the ups and downs (and I mean that literally) of being a learning-disabled, visually impaired child who experienced hyperactivity and attention problems. Thank goodness (I'm kidding) I had all kinds of other "at risk" factors too. I included all the exciting details to ensure that readers would leave grateful not to be me and sure that if I could make it, anyone can.

Chapter 14 is a resource section. Don't begin yawning yet. The information in this section is terribly exciting because it deals with getting help for your child now. It was written for every parent who has been left wondering why his or her child (the one who can tell you the meaning of life, but can't tie his shoes; the one who is really smart, but still can't read) will be called a disciplinary problem long before that child will ever be recommended for special education services. Ten-dollar phrases such as "multi-disciplinary team" will be defined, and the challenges associated with obtaining special education services will be demystified. The good news: It won't hurt a bit and you could leave with a toolbox full of suggestions and ideas that will be immediately applicable to your situation.

For those who don't have a special-needs child but are challenged by a great kid who is driving you slightly crazy—all I can say is "Welcome to parenting." I have four kids who are all set on one speed: fast. But each has different social, emotional, and learning needs. Did I mention they all move really fast? Though each child is different from every other child, my teaching and parenting experience has helped me glean useful, sound, and practical tools for raising children. I have offered my foundations for parenting hoping you will be able to take less headache medicine and enjoy your kids more.

May my story make you laugh a little and be encouraged a lot. And may the resource section of this book give you just enough advice and encouragement to enable you to dive into parenting with renewed enthusiasm and optimism about your child's future.

1

And Then There Was Me

My parents learned quickly that there is no handbook for raising a special-needs child. Doing the best they could was the order of the day. Trusting their instincts and looking for any possible solutions, they struggled toward the goal of getting me through my first few years. Amid all my failures, my mom tried to see the bright side, looking hard to find anything I was good at, teaching me even the most basic skills so I could receive some small measure of praise.

There was a lot of hand-wringing the day I was born. The chord was around my neck; my head was blue. It was a moment of crisis. "Chances are she will be fine," everyone said. While no one will ever know for sure if my learning disabilities were caused by a lack of oxygen at birth, I am convinced that as lovely as blue is, it is best if you don't start out that color.

I would like to tell you I know where it all began—where my learning issues, vision problems, and the rest came from, but the truth is, there is no perfect trail. I do know that in my family we have some fascinating people. While successful in their own right, these individuals I know and love spent many hours with dunce caps on their heads. Like me, they are a different kind of smart. They figured out ways to get through the system. They found ways to be successful in life, though most people in school would have said that their futures were, well, questionable. Dropping out of school to help out on the farm allowed them to escape and find another way. Maybe heredity played a big part in my whole "learning disabled" life story, but even if it did, we won't ever know for sure. The only thing I'm sure of is that I was not dropped on my head as a child. Well, at least no one will admit to it.

My parents got quite a dose of reality when I came home from the hospital. After having my sister, who was and is quite perfect (she could be quiet when told to do so . . . who knew?), they thought, "Hey, why not have another?" Then they got me in all my glory—so unlike my sister. Isn't that just the way of it? You have the baby that sleeps through the night and think the next one will do the same. Presto, you get a baby with colic or some other ailment that, while not life threatening, wreaks havoc on the amount of REM sleep anyone will be getting for several years.

WHEN IT RAINS, IT POURS

Well, there I was, filled with all kinds of reasons to cry. And cry I did. My back seemed to hurt for no apparent reason. Maybe it was actually my stomach that hurt. It was hard to tell. It was difficult for anyone to hold me, because I was so uncomfortable. My eyes were glassy, my nose ran, and I had ear infections, diarrhea, and colic.

There were many trips to the doctor and lots of antibiotics to cure the ear and respiratory infections that never went away. My parents and doctors thought I might be allergic to my milk-based formula, but I had so many symptoms that no one knew for sure. Switching to a soy-based version seemed to make everything worse. Was I allergic to both? My parents were exhausted, frustrated, and, dare I say, irritated, because there were no good answers to help me feel better.

At one point a doctor thought I was a gamma-globulin-deficient baby and nearly killed me with a treatment for an illness I didn't have. Oops!

Though colds, ear infections, and the like would follow me for years, it never occurred to even the most seasoned professional that I wasn't just mildly allergic to the most ordinary foods, including soy and milk. Actually I was severely allergic. While I still get a rash from fresh-cut grass and wheeze due to dust mites, I am most allergic to common foods such as oats, wheat, all forms of gluten, barley, corn, spelt, rye, food additives, onions, soy, all dairy—should I keep going? Though it is unclear if heavy antibiotic use throughout my childhood caused or at least exacerbated the problem I had with food allergies, other people in my family have similar allergies, so there may be a genetic link. We do know that if I so much as look at wheat, my ears itch. Lovely, I know. People think I am naturally thin. The truth is I am just really hungry.

Given few answers, my parents did the best they could to keep a sleepless, uncomfortable baby happy. It wasn't easy, but we all got through it. As I grew, I slept a little more and cried a little less, but I was still a handful.

With glassy eyes and a runny nose I persevered through early developmental steps at a snail's pace. I tried to roll. Nothing. I eventually would get it, but the slow start to rolling would become the story of my life when it came to movement. I was slow to crawl and never did crawl like other children. I put my elbows out in front and dragged myself. This delighted my family, because "Anything is better than nothing," they would say. Others would observe me with concerned expressions, convinced my mom was out of touch with reality as she proclaimed I was crawling when what they were seeing was obviously dragging. My mom was unfazed. I was a crawler, and nobody could tell her different.

I went from dragging to standing to walking. Not at the times I should have, but again you couldn't tell my mom that. She was just glad I was upright. But even Mom had to admit that there was something wrong with me. The dragging "thing" she chalked up to a special kind of "giftedness." She reasoned that I had developed a new way to crawl. When I stood, though, it was clear I wasn't gifted in motor coordination. I fell all the time. I fell over things, into things. I even fell up things. I was an accident waiting for a place to happen. Maybe I *was* gifted. I actually found a way to fall over things that weren't even there. I would love to tell you that everyone around me realized it wasn't just that I was uncoordinated. But my family was overwhelmed with my other issues and didn't understand that the reason I opened cabinets and hit myself in the head was that I had a *vision* problem. Well, actually, I had vision *problems* (multiple) and was hyperactive, oh and let's not forget—impulsive, uncoordinated, and fearless too! By the time I was three, I had been severely burned from placing my hand on a hot stove burner (after being told not to by a well-meaning, but dense, caregiver). I also put a coat hanger in my eye, stepped on a rusty can—after my mom pointed it out and said "Don't step there," got a concussion by placing my head under my sister as she did a walkover, and fell on the tip of the base of a rocker while someone was rocking. I had more childhood accidents than a family of 20 kids.

My parents realized there was a problem with my vision when they saw me run into a post and tell it "Excuse me" (suggesting I thought the post was a person). Soon after that, something terrible happened. One evening a drunk driver hit the car my mom and I were in. My head smashed into the steering wheel and dashboard, and I got cuts all over my forehead and left eye. Plastic surgery repaired my face, and my mom took me to an eye specialist to determine if I had any vision loss due to the accident. Mom thought I was kidding when I told the nurse in my lisping voice that I couldn't see *anything* on the chart. When the nurse left the room, my mom told me to stop this silliness. I told her I wasn't being silly. The doctor confirmed that I wasn't joking. I actually couldn't see the ducks on the chart or much of anything else. I was nearly legally blind in my left eye and missing about 25 percent of the vision in my right eye. That explained the whole falling-up-the-stairs thing.

At age three I was given a pair of glasses. The lenses were so thick there were no frames able to hold them. We eventually found a pair. A real doozy, I might add—big and brown. In addition I was diagnosed with amblyopia (lazy eye) and given a plastic patch to place over the side of my glasses covering my best eye. *What, are they crazy?* I thought. *I have one good eye, people.* But there it was: a beautiful plastic patch. The theory behind this treatment was that with my good eye covered, my bad eye would have to work extra hard. That is a swell idea in theory. In practice, well, I'm not so sure. I'm just glad I was slow, because when people called me a four-eyed pirate, I thought they were giving me a compliment.

My glasses were a big help. I could see but still had depth-perception problems combined with lack of coordination and hyperactivity. Let's just say that I hit a lot of things going really fast. I still fell and had accidents, but with glasses at least I could see everything more clearly when I hit it.

As I'm sure you've already gathered, I had what is now called attention deficit/hyperactivity disorder. Back then, there was no such diagnosis. People just called you really annoying. I talked too much, too fast, and most of what I said didn't make sense. I moved too much and too fast with no forethought. I never needed a nap. Never needed sleep. I was inattentive and distracted 24/7. I was everything you have ever thought of when you think of ADHD: impulsive, fearless (in a dangerous way like running in front of a car because it seemed like a good idea at the time), random, and impatient. I was so busy moving, there was no time to plan, think, or anticipate. The results of my misplaced random energy included broken dishes, saying the wrong things at the wrong times, moving too fast, and moving too soon. Add being uncoordinated to vision and hearing problems, and you have a recipe for disaster.

When this is who you are, you operate in your world without realizing that you are really irritating. That is, until someone (actually many people) calls you an idiot (neighborhood kids who shall go unnamed) because you don't understand knock-knock jokes. Or a relative (well-meaning I'm sure) says loudly (believing all your ear infections have actually caused deafness), "What is wrong with her?" to your mother—who stands dumbfounded, unable to answer because she is overcome by the fact that her child has just spilled red punch on ivory carpet for the fifth time in less than 20 minutes at a Christmas party.

The truth is I was okay with me. My "slowness" kind of protected me from what people said about me or to me. I got to live in my own world and I liked it there. I was itchy and anxious and moving, but when that is who you are, you don't dislike who you are, until someone suggests (millions of times, and I am not exaggerating) that you should.

Doing Something Right

By age four, pretty much everything I touched broke, and my room was a wreck. Initially my mom responded in the obvious way. She tried to make me more mainstream by training me to "fit in." She used traditional discipline such as spanking (oh, and yelling too). While it certainly got my attention, it really didn't work. You see, most of the time I wasn't intending to do something wrong, and I wasn't being openly defiant. I just thought putting shampoo all over the bathroom carpet was a good idea. Or I thought ramming my bike into our playhouse, because I didn't know how to stop, was better than landing on the neighbors' porch. I did so many things without thinking ahead. Lots of things got broken because I was simply uncoordinated and clumsy. You can't punish a kid for that, though secretly you might like to. My mom knew that spanking might be an appropriate response for some circumstances, but, in the end, I needed to be told what *to do,* not just what *not to do.* My mom knew my energy was a constant; it wasn't ever going to go away. So rather than fight it and get mad at me all the time, rather than say "Sit down and be quiet" all the time (a phrase that was said so often I thought it was my first and last name), she decided to give me something to do. Brilliant.

Mom tried to describe this new thing we were going to do. I was going to learn how to make the bed. My eyes darted all over the place. I fidgeted and bounced around. My mom stopped short, looked me in the eye, and said, "Shari, energy is good, but I don't think you are going to be able to learn how to make the bed if you have this much energy running around inside you. What do you think we can do to get rid of some of that energy?"

"Running around my head," I answered.

My mom had no idea what I was talking about, but she told me to carry on. So I got my pillow out of my bedroom and placed it in the center of the living room floor. I moved all of the living room furniture out of the way and lay on my side on the

floor with my head on the pillow. I revved up my internal
engine and began running around my head. When I had run
around my head several times, I moved the furniture back and
blew my bangs out of my eyes.

"Okay, Mom, I'm ready now," I said.

My mom replied, "Shari, you are a very good head runner. I
had no idea you could do that. But here's a little tip: Don't do it
when your grandma comes over. She won't get it." I nodded in
agreement.

Mom will tell you she was just flying by the seat of her
pants, but when you look at what she did, it was pretty clever. I
was totally disorganized, I was not really good at anything, I was
always doing the wrong thing with my energy, and I rarely got
praised for doing something right. Enter bed making. It took a
long time to learn how to make a bed. I was a little slow on the
uptake, but once I got it, I seriously made making the bed into
an art form. My mom broke it down into little steps. She had to
reteach me several times how to make the bed. When I could
do it on my own, I received praise—so seldom heard by my little
ears. It was like pixie dust. I was so excited about the idea that I
was actually doing something right, I would make the bed over
and over again just to hear my mom say I had done a good job.
The only problem was that I got so into bed making that when
my sister got up to use the bathroom in the middle of the night,
I would make the bed while she was gone.

It was obvious that I could learn, just very slowly. It also was
obvious that while not born with an innate sense of organization, I could learn organizational skills. It was also clear after

watching how I would repeat the process of bed making over and over, that repetition was soothing, and external structure created some type of internal calm. Maybe by organizing the outside, my inside felt more orderly.

Who would have guessed that bed making would change my life? But that was only the beginning. I soon learned how to do the dishes and other chores around the house. My mom would praise me, so I would keep doing the task over and over. I may have repeated tasks to the point of strangeness, but it's hard to get mad at a kid for incessant cleaning. When is the last time you said to a kid, "Could you stop washing the dishes please?"

My mom saw that even as a world-class bed maker, I still had problems. If I was interrupted while doing the dishes or some other task, I would have to start over. I may have started over because after being distracted, I forgot my place and had to return to the beginning. Or it could be that after being disrupted, it felt uncomfortable to start in the middle, so I returned to the beginning. Or it could be that I just liked the feeling of cleaning. All I know is that at the least disruption, I would start over. At first glance that doesn't seem like a big problem, but due to my high level of distractedness, no task ever got completed.

Seeing the problem, my mom suggested I talk to myself throughout tasks. If I ever got stuck after a distraction, I could talk myself through the steps of the task rather than redoing everything. Though this method worked most of the time, it was a little odd to see a four-year-old doing repetitive cleaning while talking to herself. While not something to really brag about, it is better than grape juice spilled on a white tablecloth, if you get my drift.

Soon my room was clean and the dishes were done. I needed a new cleaning chore to conquer. How could I have known that hidden in our front hall closet was the love of my life—our Hoover vacuum. I had seen it done before. My mom, my dad— they vacuumed. Wow, big deal, right? Well, until you hold the handle in your four-year-old hand and take control of a machine that can potentially suck up a Lego, you don't know what vacuuming is all about.

Let's just say that the "exterior organization creating interior calm" really kicked in with vacuuming. Our vacuum made lines on the shag rug. Does everyone know about this? I was shocked. That is where those lines were coming from. Now I was making lines and making more lines and making perfect lines. I was so concerned about perfect lines that I would walk on furniture to ensure that I didn't disrupt the perfection of my carpet lines. It made me hyperventilate when people walked on my lines. Mom sometimes had to get me a brown bag to breathe into when guests came over. To get into our house they had to walk on my lines. Arghhh!

To this day I am still making beds, doing dishes, and leaving perfect lines on shag carpet. When my husband married me, he had no idea how important lines on the shag rug were. He does now! I haven't convinced my four children, my husband, or our guests not to walk on my lines, but I secretly still hyperventilate when someone steps on our shag rug. By the way, I still talk to myself when I clean. While I still use this as a device to keep me on track amid many distractions, it could also be a sign of some type of mental stress due to having four children.

My mom had no idea what to do with her child who was up at dawn watching the test pattern on the TV. She had no great master plan to help me stop being, well, strange. What she did, though, is commendable. She loved me and took one day at a time, at every opportunity attempting to help this little bundle of inadequacies find a place in the world. With her help I became more organized—rigidly organized is more like it (more on that later)—and, in turn, more calm. I still didn't get jokes, puns, or social cues. I was still clumsy and awkward, but I could make a bed, by golly. Even though kids in the neighborhood called me names, I was unharmed by their words. I just thought they hadn't caught on to my genius.

I felt sure it was just a matter of time before I would stun the world with my unique talents of dishwashing and head running.

2

The Downside
of Different

When children are "different," it can seem as if every day offers endless challenges, ranging from finding a childcare provider to negotiating issues related to school. When there are no sure answers, faith and family offer stability to children who find little success in the world.

say this in no way to suggest that my mom thought less of one child than another, but it is on the record that she had to adjust her expectations of me quite often. While she watched my sister dress herself and get ready each day, she in turn hoped I might one day put my shoes on the right feet. While my sister spoke French and English quite well, my mom hoped I might one day be able to speak coherently and without a lisp and stutter.

While Mom might have once hoped I'd rule the world, maybe better goals included living on my own and holding a job.

While other people would whisper about me and wonder why I was odd, my mom had to hold her head high and hope that running around your head might become an Olympic sport.

I had a long list of oddities presenting such a contrast to my sibling that my mom wondered if I had been switched at birth. Just beyond the concern for my overall health and whether I would stay upright long enough to walk in a straight line came other developmental milestones having to do with thinking and processing. While there were early signs that I was slow, as each day passed it became clear it wasn't just a learning-style difference; there were actual intellectual problems.

While not necessarily a red flag if presented in isolation, several things gave my mom pause when it came to the way I functioned. If witnessed today, even at an age preceding school, some of these characteristics or preferences would suggest to a parent and/or educator that a learning disability or other issue might be present. Back then most people just thought I was a little off.

- I didn't like to color due to motor coordination and attention issues.
- I found it difficult to hold a pencil, crayon, or marker and use it to write, draw, or color.
- I couldn't snap my fingers, button a button, clap my hands, hit a ball, or tie my shoe.
- I couldn't tell my left hand from my right hand, understand the difference between north, south, east, and west, or understand directions related to north, south, east, and west or right and left.
- I couldn't recognize numbers or letters.

- I couldn't attach meaning to numbers and letters.
- I couldn't repeat what was said to me, remember sequences, or understand and follow directions.
- I was slow to speak, and when I did speak, what I said didn't make sense.
- I spoke fast and was impulsive, often saying things that were incoherent and even insensitive simply because I spoke before thinking.
- I spoke with a lisp and a stutter (both more pronounced when I was under pressure).
- I couldn't explain what I meant, tell or retell a story, pay attention, or follow a line of reasoning.
- I couldn't do puzzles of any kind or games that required spatial or sequential understanding.
- I didn't enjoy art projects, cooking, or any other project that required motor coordination, following directions and/or reading.
- I didn't like playing almost any type of game including board, dice, or card games.
- I played alone because I was viewed as irritating, inattentive, and impulsive.
- I didn't understand jokes, puns, or social cues.
- Ear infections had left me hard-of-hearing, so I couldn't always understand what I heard.
- Even if I heard what was being said to me I did not often interpret the information correctly. If someone said to me, "5, 6, 7," I might hear, "7, 6, 5" or "6, 5, 7." It was hard to repeat and act on information that I heard incorrectly.

- I had trouble understanding what I was hearing and discriminating between words being spoken and other noises in a room.
- While my vision improved with the intervention of glasses, I was still unable to track lines of words on a page and had great difficulty with depth perception.
- Letters and numbers often moved and/or jumped on the page, making it even more difficult to track.
- Reversals of numbers and letters were commonplace.
- Seeing things backward went even beyond symbols and words. I put my shoes on the wrong feet and for many years thought they looked right that way.
- Sensory integration problems were obvious immediately. I had difficulty receiving and interpreting sound, light, and movement. I seemed to receive all input into my senses with no pattern or order. It made me feel, and even look, overwhelmed and disoriented.
- Even my skin experienced sensory overload. I seldom found clothing comfortable. My skin felt itchy, uncomfortable, and intolerant of different textures.
- Though wishing for physical attention like a hug from my mom or wrestling with my dad, my body didn't know what to do with all the sensory stimulation. Even a hug made me feel uncomfortable and overwhelmed, so I would withdraw and/or become stiff to try to prevent overload.
- The brighter the light in a room, especially fluorescent, the more I had trouble concentrating. Bright light also

aggravated all of my dyslexia symptoms such as reversals, omissions, and tracking problems. It caused teachers and others concern when I demonstrated a preference for being in the dark or, at the very least, in dim light most of the time, but I was calmer and able to function better in lower light.

- I didn't operate well in noisy, chaotic environments, and yet I seemed to seek stimulation, often vying to be right in the middle of everything.

- I tended to repeat tasks, as if anxious that I hadn't done them right.

- I would repeatedly ask the same question, as if I had forgotten the answer.

- I had to be taught basic skills over and over, and even then I might not retain the information.

- Even the most basic skill needed to be broken down into smaller parts for me to understand how to replicate it.

- Due to my high energy level, I had a tendency to be anxious and jittery. I rocked for hours before I could go to sleep, and I had to rub my feet or hands together to calm myself. During the day I used rocking, or bouncing my foot, knee, or hand, in an effort to "get the energy out."

- I did not transition well from one activity to another. I would become anxious and frustrated if I had to stop what I was doing to leave or do something else. It was as if something being "undone" left me internally uneasy and uncomfortable.

- Though there was only a hint of it initially, repetitive cleaning would soon become obsessive-compulsive behavior. Even at ages three and four I used cleaning to address anxiety. (I would have simply said it made me calm down.) If I was under stress, I would clean. The more internal or external anxiety I experienced, the more I would clean. Obsessive behavior moved beyond cleaning to hand washing and other repetitive behaviors.

DIFFERENTLY-ABLED IS JUST PLAIN DIFFERENT WHEN YOU ENTER SCHOOL

I was so different that it kept my mom awake at night. Not knowing her secret worries about me, I just kept making beds and doing the things that worked, and managed to get by, still unaware of what the real world thought. Because I was politely and not-so-politely turned away from neighborhood games, I concentrated on solitary activities. I rode my bike while sporting multicolored bruises and variously-sized bumps as trophies of the landmarks I had hit. I made mud pies in the woods and played with our cats. There were also many hours spent in my room listening to Disney records. I could listen to the records again and again and be entertained. For an inattentive kid, this was unique. Though also entertaining, storybook records, music, and even television also proved useful tools. Background noise helped focus my mind. It brought down the internal noise in my head by giving my brain something to focus on. It was usual for me to have the TV or record player going, even if I wasn't actually paying attention, because it was better than dealing with the static in my head.

Mom learned that I could sing by listening at my door hearing me try to re-create what I heard on my records. Even with a lisp and a stutter I could stay on pitch and mimic what I heard. Capitalizing on my ability to sing, my mom encouraged me to share my gift at every family get-together. Maybe she thought it would distract me from policing my vacuum lines as guests entered and exited our home. God bless her for trying. People were kind enough to endure my home talent shows, but let's face it, you can only listen to someone lisp "Somewhere Over the Rainbow" so many times.

In spite of all my home successes with cleaning and singing, there was no room for me in the real world. The neighbor kids shunned me and relatives whispered about me. My mom secretly hoped I would suddenly change; like magic I would fit in. But it was not to be. Just when my mom thought I couldn't get any further out of the mainstream, I went to school.

What? Where were the carpets to vacuum? Where were the dishes to wash? None of the talents I had were needed (or wanted) at school. When I couldn't display my vast array of skills, I found other things to consume my time. Being impulsive and inattentive really gets you noticed in preschool. While I thought I was *popular* because my name was mentioned all the time, the other kids and my teacher would have chosen other words to describe my standing in the class.

When you are hyper and impulsive it never occurs to you that getting out of your seat while the teacher is in the middle of a lesson is a bad idea. Touching other people and making weird noises also seems like a good idea. If getting out of your seat or touching people around you doesn't get you noticed, there is always raising your hand, even though you have nothing to say. The teacher was not amused by my antics. I didn't understand that when she had an angry expression on her face and was physically putting me in my chair, it was because of something I did. I just thought she was having a bad day.

Most of my preschool year was spent at the back of the class with my head down on the table (a form of punishment). Recess was the only "subject" that really worked for me. No one played with me (big surprise), but at least I wasn't being asked to sit down and be quiet. I think we all know the whole "sit down and be quiet" thing doesn't really work for me. (The irony is now people pay me to stand up and speak! Parents, try to remember that when your child is driving you crazy.)

While I lived in la-la land believing the teacher was frustrated with someone other than me, my mom was getting an earful on a daily basis. "Shari won't sit still. Shari won't be quiet. Shari won't pay attention. Shari does things without thinking. Like when she walked out the school door and onto a busy street looking for a lost plastic turtle!" My mom wanted to defend me on that last one. I mean, after all, it was a prized possession, one of a pair that belonged to a Noah's ark set I got as part of a gas station promotion (buy so many gallons and you get another pair of animals). Who wouldn't risk life and limb to preserve such a toy? As always, my mom had to say *blah, blah, blah* in her head while the teacher spoke, so she wouldn't say something she regretted. "You're right!"

my mom wanted to shout (or at least say loudly). "You're right. Shari is—to put it mildly—different. Now that we have established that fact, what are we going to do about it?"

Yes, it is true. She was asking the one-million-dollar question: What to do with Shari? Unfortunately, no one had an answer to that question. We were living in a different time from today. Not only did people have less information about how to diagnose and treat learning disabilities, there were no laws to govern how we referred, diagnosed, and placed children with special needs. A low IQ test and inadequate performance in regular education, and you were either placed in a self-contained classroom or removed from public education. Parents were often left on a lonely journey of helping their children themselves, finding help for their children outside the public schools, or succumbing to low expectations or even institutionalization.

I'm sure my preschool teacher didn't hold out any hope that I would suddenly understand what she was trying to teach, but no doubt she dreamed I would drop out, move away, or at the very least stop being irritating. It is doubtful that anyone (except my mom) was actually losing sleep over my behavior issues and lackluster performance in every subject area including finger painting, because, well, it was just preschool. It was easy to say, "She may catch up," then politely pass me off the next year so I could become someone else's problem. I do know that my teacher didn't recommend holding me back for another year of preschool. While no one was ready to throw in the towel after my preschool experience, there were plenty of signs that my early experiences in the public schools would be fraught with challenges.

Foundation of Hope

It wouldn't be long before I would fit into every "at risk" category except English as a second language. But in my early years, even with all the challenges in my life, I was blessed with a few important safety nets, even as a four-eyed pirate catches a break now and then.

Though my parents didn't stay together forever, I was fortunate that my parents were married during my early life. My life at school would become increasingly stressful, and knowing I had a relatively stable home life was important. Even if my parents were not getting along, I considered myself lucky to have a mom and a dad. Of even greater importance than my parents' marital stability was the fact that they took me to church.

I accepted the Lord early because I was told at church that I could. It was just that simple. One day I got up from the daily nap I never took (though I did go into my room and pretend to nap because Mom begged me to). "Mom, you'll never gueth what I did," I announced.

Thinking I had cut my doll's hair and poured perfume on its head (and the carpet) again, my mom said cautiously, "Shari, what did you do?"

I said, "I let Jethus into my heart."

She said, "You did?"

I said, "Yep!"

"How did you do that?" Mom asked.

"I just lifted up my underthirt and he came right in!" I said with a big grin.

Who needs a nap when you can be saved? By the way, I would be saved many times after that. No one ever told me you only needed to do it once. It felt so good, I got saved often. From the Little Red Barn (a storytelling venue at county fairs) to the local Billy Graham crusade, I was always the one raising my hand when the question was asked, "Does anyone want to accept the Lord?"

Throughout my life I was going to need a bigger friend than anyone on this earth could be. While my faith may have been imperfect, it never wavered. I knew that even if I was physically abandoned by family and friends, I was never truly alone. I knew that there was someone watching out for me to whom I was accountable. In the early days of my faith, though, it was just about the joy of knowing God and believing I was special.

While God may have accepted me with an abundance of mercy, babysitters were not so forgiving. The truth is I scared a lot of them away. I would like to believe some of them were not stable to begin with, and that is why they ran screaming from our home (a slight exaggeration, but not by much). But the truth is, people didn't know what to do with me. When my mom returned to work, I was three years old. I could wash a dish and sing you a song, but most people didn't get me.

Before Mom started work, she advertised for a caregiver who would come to our home. She was smart enough to know that going to another environment was probably not going to work for me. Whose bed would I make? Mrs. Sager came to work for our family after answering our ad. She was a lovely person and cared about me very much. I was sick a lot and she took good care of me. I was annoying, but she was willing to overlook it. She often told my mom to disregard what other people said about me because she knew I would be okay. She was a godly person, and to this day I believe she had a direct line to God. Everything she ever told my mom about me eventually came true.

My parents' marriage, the Lord, and my caregiver Mrs. Sager formed a triangle that created a foundation for me in my early life. One other blessing came from an unlikely place, though—a dilapidated cabin with green siding and a rickety staircase at a tiny beach called Warm Beach. This funky little place became my hideaway. There I marched in a local parade as a pillow person (don't ask; pillow people are hard to explain) and won a "best of fair" ribbon for a loaf of bread in the county fair. While I didn't like to bake, my mother discovered kneading bread was a good pastime for a hyperactive kid. Little did we know that the bread, which never should have risen due to the beating it received from my little fists, won over recipes that had been passed down from generation to generation. I'm telling you, there was something magical about this place.

While I didn't have any friends up at the beach, I did become well acquainted with the on-call staff at the local emergency room where I ended up often, thanks to a variety of ailments and accidents such as being bitten by a poisonous spider. There are very few poisonous spiders in Washington State, but all of them found me. Oh, and falling down a flight of stairs with my bike. Don't ask how this happened. I mean, do you really want to know why I was going down a steep flight of stairs carrying a bike?

Even with new scars resulting from my time at the beach, I found our cabin to be an oasis that would become even more important to me as my life became more turbulent.

3

The First Day of School and Other Scary Stories

As a parent it is easy to believe "experts" can foretell the future and there is no way your child can achieve beyond bleak assessments for his or her future. My story is all about how a determined mom and resourceful teachers turned the tables on the "inevitable" and searched for ways to not let test scores and limitations have the last word.

I didn't have to worry much about the first few days of kindergarten. I didn't go. I was actually excited about going to school, but my body wasn't cooperating. Though it was usually an ear infection, bronchitis, or some other upper respiratory ailment involving a lot of phlegm that kept me home, hives and a stomachache caused my absences this time.

My mom hovered over me, looking at the welts rising on my skin the minute leaving for school was mentioned. She asked if I was afraid or worried about school. I said, "No," and even believed it. Mom wasn't buying it though. She kept asking if I was afraid until, frankly, I started to wonder if I *should* be afraid. I mean, what could happen at kindergarten? Then it all became clear. I heard my sister mention something about nap time. I was shocked. *Nap time in kindergarten? What, are they trying to kill me?* I thought. Upon hearing about this so-called "nap time," I no longer cared if I ever attended kindergarten. My hives suddenly got much worse.

Eventually, even my red, itchy welts couldn't keep me home. I went to school swelling, but eager nonetheless. I knew there weren't any beds to make, but I held out hope that kindergarten would be better than preschool.

Once at school, nap time was endured but never actually taken. I watched the kids around me succumb to slumber on their mats. I was in agony—up since 4:00 A.M. and still filled with energy. I saw my classmates as sellouts for falling for this whole scam, but I kept my mind set on recess—the only *real* highlight of my day.

When in class, I was often caught daydreaming, falling off my chair, or bouncing my knee to an unknown beat in my head. Being unable to sustain attention, follow directions, and perform basic skills made me a target for criticism. The negative words were still not jarring, though. I took them in stride but found myself often wanting to leave the room. I made my escape in a small bathroom at the back of our class. I spent a lot of time there, but not because I had to go to the bathroom. It was just a good place to hide when my teacher started talking about numbers and letters. I got away with it for a while, but my mom finally was told of my extended stays in the washroom, and I soon lost permission to go to the bathroom during school hours unless it was clearly an emergency.

Once out of the bathroom, I was left to fall back on the old, faithful devices I used to get by before: being out of my seat, touching people, and raising my hand for no apparent reason. My teacher became increasingly frustrated with my behavior. She was considering retirement, and I was quickly hastening her departure. My mom made many trips to school to put out brush fires I had caused. All the while, I kept waiting for my chance to shine. Then it came. Little did everyone know that along with my advanced skills in dishwashing, I could also save people.

LEADER OF THE MISFITS

As you already know, I was unable to grasp the subtleties of life such as realizing that when someone called me names it wasn't a good thing. I couldn't get in touch with my own feelings or understand which ones to have and when, but I was oddly hypersensitive to other people in pain. A kid crying on the playground acted like a homing device for me. I always seemed to find them. Seeing someone in distress suddenly made me feel like a superhero ready to save the day.

Some kids actually pushed me away when I offered help. I guess they saw my glasses and runny nose and felt they were better off on their own. I was resilient, though, and kept trying until I found someone who needed me.

Often the child had fallen or was hurt in some way, and that child would pour out his or her heart through sobs of pain. I'd listen as intently as an inattentive hyperactive kid can. Sometimes due to their sobbing, and sometimes due to my slowness, I didn't understand what they were saying. I just knew they were hurting. In these situations I could rise up easily and offer a shoulder to cry on or a word of advice.

The problem is, I don't think my advice was very good. I was still trying to determine if jumping off a ten-foot rockery for a cookie was a good idea, but some people took it anyway. I actually convinced one little girl who was scared of a bully to walk home with me—a couple of miles in a different direction from her home! Her mom was terrified when she didn't return home after school. My mom was mortified when I showed up with a little girl in tow she had never seen before. I said, "Mom, Jane is afraid of a bully tho I brought her home with me." It was hard for Mom to be angry. I was just trying to help. The little girl's mom was not so forgiving. After this incident, my mom told me I should not bring anyone home with me from school without their parent's permission. I agreed to refrain from picking up strays and decided to stick with what I knew: the Bible.

I would bring the "Good Book" to school and tell people, "I don't know how to read, but thith book will save your life." Most of the little underdogs and misfits I was reaching out to didn't really want to accept Christ on the monkey bars but were just glad to have someone come along that wasn't throwing rocks at them. It wasn't long before I had a small group of converts willing to put up with my preaching just to have a friend.

I was a kid whose nose ran most of the time. And I think we all know how attractive mucous is. When you are the "booger kid," you don't exactly get your pick of friends. But I had a group of faithful followers willing to overlook my boogers because I overlooked my friends' faults (like smelling bad). You think I'm kidding, but I'm not. One of my best friends was a boy named Bobby. He smelled bad. His last name was Stinks. I'll let that sink in for a minute. My glasses and patch were looking really good at this point. Another one of my friends was Glenna. She was very overweight and had hair like a Brillo pad. At home alone until late into the night, she sat by herself eating Captain Crunch and slept in a chair with a lamp shade on her head because she was scared of the dark. I tried this method, but it didn't ward off the boogie monster; it just left a dent on my forehead. Then there was Janie. She was the little girl so afraid of a bully that she walked home with me. Her mom didn't want her to be friends with me after the whole "accidental kidnapping" episode, but Janie defied that admonition, unless her mom was around. Then Janie pretended not to know me. While not fiercely loyal, these were my people and I their self-appointed leader.

HOW TO SUCCEED IN FIRST GRADE WITHOUT REALLY TRYING

Nowadays people expect kids to be reading by the end of kindergarten. Whew! Am I glad to be middle-aged. According to today's standards, I would never have been moved to first grade. Thankfully, due to the existing standard there was still a chance to learn to read in the coming year, so I was promoted to first grade.

Same song, second and third verses. I thought any moment people would discover my greatness. Though I was starting to lose faith in these teachers who couldn't see how special I was, I was willing to give them another chance. I mean, now they had the whole day with me. Let's just say it didn't take long for my first-grade teacher to see how special I was. We just had different definitions of the word.

On the first day of school I had great intentions. I was really going to show off my skills. And I did. I ran in, slid to a stop (make a screeching noise here for effect), and sat down right in front. I thought, *Why bother one person when you can bother everyone here?* The teacher was busy doing something and had no idea of my power of persuasion. I managed to get all the kids in the class to stomp their feet wildly on the newly waxed floor. Apparently, these kids didn't know me, because seldom did anyone but my misfit buddies ever do anything I said or did.

With the clattering of little feet all around and me grinning from ear to ear at my accomplishment, I turned around to observe my followers. What I didn't know was the teacher was standing over me ready to strike. I mean that literally. I felt a clunk on the head. I thought, *Hey, that felt like metal.* It was. It was the teacher's pen, and the teacher's pen and I became very close friends. All the kids in class suddenly became quite discerning about me. Funny how seeing someone get clunked on the head will do that to you. For the rest of the year I was pretty much invisible to them.

As you can see, my hopes of being noticed in first grade came true rather quickly, though once again I was noticed for all the wrong reasons. Within two weeks I had been reprimanded a zillion times for unspeakable acts such as going to the water fountain five times during a reading lesson and being unable to keep my hands to myself. Oh, and I never stopped talking. I actually told the people I was touching that I was touching them. Like they didn't know! My teacher moved me from my selected seat in the front row back a little ways. Then back a few more rows, until, finally, I was behind a partition at an isolation desk. Still I managed to get attention. Soon I was out in the hallway facing a wall for significant portions of the day. My teacher, at her wit's end, decided to have me tested for learning disabilities. Smart move, don't you think?

My parents came to the meeting and all my tests were laid out on a table. This was before IEPs (Individualized Education Plans) and Multidisciplinary Teams (teams of specially trained individuals gathered as a group to determine placement for special-needs children). My parents were told that I had auditory, visual, and motor challenges. My mom whispered to my dad, "I hope they didn't spend a lot on the tests, because we could have told them that." Based on my current in-class performance and the results of my tests, it was determined that the best place for me was special education class. I would still spend non-instruction time in regular education, but I would learn basic skills in another room. My parents had no problem with the suggestion of special education. If anything, I think their response was, finally!

THEY FINALLY SEE IT

When she told me I was going to a special classroom, my teacher probably said, "special education." All I heard was, "special."

I thought, *They finally see it. Of course. I am so elevated in my skills that they had to create a special room just for me.* I already knew I was special. I mean, how many people do you know who organize their sock drawer several times in one day and still put on mismatched socks? But I was taken aback when some of my misfit friends, and a few kids I had not seen before, lined up at the door behind me, ticking and twitching away. I had no idea why this group had assembled to go to my special classroom, but I looked at this group moving involuntarily and looking odd, and I thought, *That is tho thad. You juth got to feel thorry for them.* I decided (without being elected, mind you) that I should be their leader. I mean, who better?

With me at the head of the line, we marched to the other end of the school. This was when special education classes were often located in the unventilated part of the building. We were lucky our room actually had windows. They just didn't open because they were painted shut and covered with dark green paint—an ingenious method for preventing distractions among kids who were highly entertained by watching the wind blow. I refused to see the green paint as a negative, though. I assumed the windows were blocked because the administration of my school didn't want the other kids to get jealous after witnessing the special treatment we would receive in our special classroom.

We had a great teacher. I mean she was *great*—very patient and kind. It was her first year. Eeek! I wonder at what point during my year with her that she reconsidered her career choice. Tony Schlone was a great teacher because she cared very much. Her classroom was warm and safe. Though I didn't learn how to read or to do any of the basic skills required of me that year, I loved going to school. That is why she was a great teacher; she kept me coming back. As long as I was there, she had a chance.

The Joke's On Me

For me, the most difficult part of going to special education was getting there. At the beginning of the day we would hang up our coats in regular ed, get in line, and make the long walk to our classroom. I call it a "long walk" not just because the room was on the other side of the school, but because, inevitably, we would encounter kids passing us on their way to the library or gym and insults would fly. Initially, I would laugh along with the name-calling, partly because I didn't understand what they were saying and partly because it seemed better than saying nothing.

Returning the insult wasn't an option for me. I'd like to tell you it was because of my high moral standards, but it was because I was too slow to think of something to say. I tried to respond to an insult once. It went something like this:

Big kid with an attitude: "Hey, retard, are you on your way to the retard class?"

Me: "Oh, yeah . . . (long pause) . . . well, yeah!"

I'm sure you can see the problem. Laughing along with an insult actually caused great frustration on the part of the person insulting me. What do you do when the person you have just called "retard" laughs and says, "Thank you"? It isn't very satisfying. Laughing along with the bullies proved to be my best defense.

Eventually, though, even my slowness couldn't protect me. While I may not have been making great strides academically, developmentally I was beginning to wake up. Even with a below-average IQ I was becoming aware that I was infamous, not famous, at school and that being in a "special" class wasn't because I was special. My mom saw how kids treated me in the neighborhood and got reports from my sister about countless incidents on the school playground. Even though I had hearing loss, I could now hear people whisper about me. It is strange how you can go from laughing it off to being self-conscious to the point of inhibition. My descent into low self-esteem began early, halfway through my first-grade year. It is sad too, because until then I was rather bubbly in an annoying sort of way, but bubbly nonetheless. I started to contemplate dropping out—yes, dropping out of first grade. I'm not sure you can actually do that, but I was thinking about it.

While some people would have sought counseling or searched for medical intervention to ward off the self-esteem issues creeping up on me, my mom did her best to create home-made inspiration and motivation to lift my spirits. Since she didn't anticipate that I would be rewarded for outstanding grades or behavior at school anytime soon, she created awards—plaques and signs indicating that I was the best "bed maker," "drawer organizer," and "line maker." She also wrote notes on napkins and put them in my lunch box. The notes offered praise and compliments. I don't know if anyone is interested, but we now have research results to indicate how long a Scott napkin will last if preserved in a 1970s photo album. I not only didn't wipe my face or hands on the napkins, I actually saved them in an album. Words of praise are powerful!

NOWHERE TO GO BUT OUT

By the end of my first-grade year my parents were told I could no longer stay in the public schools and should be institutionalized. Furthermore, based on my academic nonperformance so far, it was suggested that I was unlikely ever to be educated beyond the fifth or sixth grade. I would like to tell you that everyone was wrong, but I had a below-average IQ and severe learning disabilities, among other things. I can see how it was easy for people to look at my tests and my lack of ability, and assume the worst.

Thankfully, after a good cry and some soul-searching Mom decided to disregard the bleak assessment of my future and ask for help. She didn't want me institutionalized. Her fear was that in an institution or residential school people might believe I would only reach a certain level, and I would not be encouraged to reach beyond it. Out of desperation she reached out to a teacher she barely knew and begged her to keep me the next year. This teacher would have to do so without the help of any special services, mind you. Because the administration felt I was not suited for the public schools, she would have to take me on as her special project and, essentially, prove that I could stay. She agreed. Why she took me, I will never know, but because of her I got another chance.

4

Class Clown or Learning Disabled: You Be the Judge

It didn't take long for a kid like me to give up hope on any kind of success in school. While I resigned myself to being good at falling off my chair, a teacher who could have given up long before refused to let the fact that I couldn't read and write stop her from trying to teach me. Her effort should remind us all to never lose hope, even if progress is slow.

Would you be surprised if I told you that even with a dedicated caring teacher, I still didn't learn how to read or do other basic skills my second-grade year? It was like treading water for a whole year, except there was no pool. The good news: Miss Derek didn't hit me on the head with a pen, always a positive. But when not getting hit on the head with a pen is the highlight of the year, it isn't a good situation.

I simply didn't understand school. I didn't understand what people were trying to teach me. I didn't understand, at least some of the time (though it was becoming clearer), why I irritated people. I kept wondering: *If you can't do even the simplest things that you are asked to do, why should you keep coming back every day?* I'm sure every teacher who had taught me so far was wondering the same thing. But there I was.

With my role as "least likely to succeed" pretty well secured, I began to view school as a black hole that was swallowing me. I would mark the days off like a jail sentence on my monthly school lunch calendar. "Another turkey gravy day gone," I would say with a victorious swipe of my washable marker.

I think prior to this time I was disruptive in class because I was impulsive and random. I didn't have an agenda, just too much energy. I was aware that teachers seemed to get upset (an understatement) by my behavior, though I wasn't always completely sure why. However, after you get hit on the head a few times and spend extended periods of time in a cubicle at the back of the room, it starts to become clear that the teacher is mad at you, and your behavior might be the issue. In my little mind, though, I was thinking, *I am who I am. I don't think I can change. Maybe I even won't change. I mean, excuse me, but at home my mom says I'm great. While no one else thinks so, my mom has informed me the rest of the world is wrong.*

What a dilemma. People don't like you, but you don't think it is possible to change. Or maybe what they don't like about you is the very thing that either makes you who you are or is part of what you think makes you interesting. What do you do? What I did was to split myself. At school I got through. At home I made beds.

It is interesting, though, what "getting through at school" really means. For me it meant becoming really good at distracting people. This technique isn't for the faint-of-heart, though. You have to be willing to get in trouble, but the result is that you might get a laugh, or if nothing else, you might get to avoid sitting through a phonics lesson. Okay, so you end up in the hall, but it's better to be the kid in trouble than the kid who can't read. The energy I used to clean at home was put to good use leaning back in my chair and "accidentally" falling on the floor with great dramatic flare. I expanded my repertoire of antics to include raising my hand, waving it wildly, and yelling, "beep-beep." A surefire hit with everyone but the teacher! Oh, and let's not forget asking obvious questions repeatedly.

Developed out of a necessity due to hearing and learning issues, asking repetitive questions was elevated to a higher status when I saw how it got a rise out of my classmates.

"What do you mean when you say, 'Put your name at the top of the paper'?" I would ask in all seriousness.

Miss Derek would say, "Well, Shari, it means putting your name on the top line of the paper." Then she would go to the board, draw a sheet of paper, and demonstrate. Because my questions should have been followed by the word, "Duh," an eruption of laughter resulted, fueling me to continue. Sometimes I'd add a "stupid comment" to ensure maximum disruption.

After listening to my teacher read *The Tortoise and the Hare*, I held up a lock of my hair and announced loudly, "My hair has never won a race and never will." Laughter from the kids, grimace from my teacher. It was worth it. I touched people, made weird noises, and went to the water fountain and bathroom at least 50 times a day to ensure that I got enough exercise and that no one left school without a good laugh.

While thinking I was really putting one over on Miss Derek, I learned she had the situation well in hand. Though Iris Derek may have looked shy and retiring, she actually had the constitution of a drill sergeant. She was a no-nonsense kind of gal, but she had a soft heart beneath her '70s polyester plaid dress.

Having been a teacher for many years, she had perfected the don't-smile-until-November rule. Oh, and did I mention she had eyes in the back of her head, had supersonic hearing, and (much like a comic book hero) could be in several places at once and stretch her arms long distances to take things out of unsuspecting children's hands and tap their shoulders when they were doing things they weren't supposed to? She also had perfected a sweet, gentle hold she would use on out-of-control students, a hold which could be intensified to death-grip status when the situation warranted it. Not that I would know, of course. She was a one-woman army perfect for the likes of me.

I came into her class ready to be mediocre. On the first day, the girl who used to run to get a front-row seat slipped into a chair at the back of the class. I had assumed my role. I could see the future. I felt I would be looking at the backs of people's heads for the rest of my life, and while not the best view, it was becoming comfortable.

Miss Derek saw me melting into my seat in the back of the class and knew it was a matter of time before I couldn't be revived.

GETTING MY ATTENTION AND OTHER AMAZING FEATS

One day, a short time into the year, I was caught unaware. I walked to my seat and was swiftly told by Miss Derek that this was no longer where I would be sitting.

"What?" I said, with a healthy dose of indignation.

Miss Derek repeated her previous statement, "This is no longer where you will be sitting. I have changed the seating chart." Da da da da! The beginning of Beethoven's Fifth began playing in my head. Though I heard what she said, I hoped she was kidding.

So I replied, with more indignation and a tremendous amount of wit, "Huh?"

Trying to be patient, but realizing I wasn't going to go willingly to a place where (the previous year) pens came out of thin air and hit me on the head, Miss Derek took me by the arm and led me to a desk in the front row by her desk. I got that sweaty, prickly feeling people often get when they have been tricked.

How could this be? I was doing great in the back of the room. I couldn't see well or hear clearly, but in terms of shuffling my feet, I was at the top of my game. Surely Miss Derek didn't think I could actually learn. I mean, check my permanent file, people. Hello?

Not going to happen! I was soon to discover that Miss Derek was not planning to subscribe to the Shari-can't-learn newsletter.

Moving me to the front row was just the beginning of my teacher's diabolical scheme. Soon she would expect me to actually stay in my seat for more than five minutes. *What?* Now when I rose to go to the water fountain for a much-needed escape, my shoulder was met with a firm hand guiding me back into my chair. All the while she kept talking as if nothing had happened. Not one to give up, I employed other strategies, such as waiting until she turned to the blackboard, to once again get out of my seat. But like mothers who become ambidextrous and appear to move as if they lack shoulder cartilage as they wildly swat at misbehaving kids in the backseat of the car, Miss Derek's hand always found her way to me.

It wasn't long before her omnipresent hand was used for other effective strategies. I would be fully immersed in the important activity of touching my thumbs on each finger of my hands with a quickening pace or rolling my tongue (a genetic gift given to but a few) when a sudden sharp tap on my desktop awakened me to my teacher's presence. While the crack of her pen sounded better on the desk than my skull, it was irritating to never reach the peak intensity of thumb touching. Without exaggerating, I have to tell you it was not only difficult to pull away from being tuned out and break away from mindless repetitive behaviors, it felt almost physically painful to shift gears. It would often take several strikes of her pen on my desk before I had fully returned to reality.

Coming to, I would find my class rhythmically speaking the

sounds of letters and reciting corresponding words. I made every attempt to shake off my sense of disorientation and look at Miss Derek. When my eyes finally met hers, she gave me a stern look, which suggested that if I didn't stop rolling my tongue and start paying attention, my life might be over. No need for Ritalin here; I'm focused. Once my mind was back in the room, I tried to go along with the chorus of other kids but was not fully aware of what we were doing. Still, to be paying attention even a little was actually progress. A touch on the shoulder, a tap on the desk, a hand reminding me to stay seated—Miss Derek kept at it in hopes I would pay attention even for a few minutes of each lesson.

Still, though, you can look like you are paying attention but be a really good faker. I was pretty good at the fake pay-attention look. Nod your head and mouth the word "Yes" to suggest you know what is going on. All the while your mind is darting randomly to obscure thoughts and meaningless drivel. Miss Derek even had an answer for this one: Call on students randomly and make them recite what has just been said. What would she think of next? "Repeat what I just said to the person next to you." That's a good one. "Say it out loud to yourself." Even better! Write it, say it, sing it, build it, draw it, tell a friend, tell yourself. You name the strategy and my teacher probably tried it. While not used to benefit only me, these strategies were making a difference in my ability to focus and remain tuned in.

As she addressed my inattentiveness, Miss Derek also had to aggressively address my need for movement before my classmates staged a revolt. My natural inclination was to do things that were—to put it bluntly—highly irritating, but Miss Derek wouldn't stand for it. Drumming a pencil on the table or fingers on the inside of my desk were my favorite ways to release nervous energy, and don't get me started on the merits of tapping my shoes on the floor. I quickly learned that my need to move did not supersede my teacher's need for quiet. If I did anything disruptive, I got a healthy dose of Miss Derek.

It always came as a surprise, though, how my noise was terminated. I'd be completely involved playing percussion on the table with my pencil when suddenly my hand would be left vacant. *Where did my drumstick go?* I'd wonder. That is how fast she was. She was able to strike like lightning, removing objects from my hand in a matter of seconds or flattening my hand on the desk in a flash, quickly silencing my instrument.

With most of my movement options labeled no-no's, I was left to develop my knee-bouncing technique at a competitive level. While not my first choice, knee-bouncing was an excellent way to release energy and an endless source of entertainment; the problem is it makes you look like you are "detoxing" or having some type of small ongoing seizure. I never got in trouble for it, though. I think my teacher understood my need for repetitive movement, so as long as it didn't disrupt other people, she let me have at it. On a side note, over time I did learn never to knee-bounce in a row of chairs that were connected. Students in my row often mistook aggressive knee movement as the beginnings of an earth tremor.

Having curbed my enthusiasm for playing bongos on my desk, I still tended to get attention by goofing off. Miss Derek employed a sinister strategy to extinguish this behavior. Instead of telling me to stop a particular behavior, she gave me something to do. What kind of mastermind was I dealing with? I had been very comfortable hearing, "Stop it!" or the ever-popular, "Knock it off!" The problem was—if I wasn't going to do irritating or repetitive behaviors, what was I going to do?

Miss Derek began having me hand out papers and perform other small tasks in our classroom. Some tasks, such as passing out papers, did cause me to hit a few bumps. I didn't know how to read all the names on the papers, which seems kind of important, but apparently not crucial because Miss Derek let me do it anyway. The other kids spent a lot of time exchanging papers, but I still felt good about myself. Giving me something to do proved to be a powerful approach. Doing something with your energy that is good (even if you do it slightly wrong), and getting praised for it, beats falling off your chair. I still had to sit in my seat sometimes, but Miss Derek understood I couldn't stay there for long. Now instead of going to the water fountain, I got to clean desks. When I did have to sit down, there was quite a lot of redirecting, but knowing I soon would be able to get out of my seat to bang erasers gave me hope.

Miss Derek kind of scared me, but in a good way. I didn't want to feel her death grip on my shoulder anytime soon, but if it came my way, I could take it because I knew somewhere behind those glasses she cared about me. I mean, come on; she let me file for her. What was she thinking? I couldn't tell the difference between a "b" and a "d" and she was letting me file for her. I'm sure she's still trying to figure out what happened. The good news is because Miss Derek showed that she trusted me and believed in me, I began to like going to school. Don't tell anyone, but I actually looked forward to it.

It wasn't long before I became a class monitor. What a genius that Miss Derek was. The year before, my teacher had several people monitoring me! Ah, but my teacher knew that putting me in a position of responsibility was risky (Gee, do ya think?) but necessary. If I was a helper, she reasoned, maybe I wouldn't be such a troublemaker. Her plan worked.

My responsibilities as class monitor were very complicated and required tremendous skill (according to me). I was in charge of leading lines, a job I thought required a high level of security clearance. At first I didn't know if I was up to the task. Then I remembered that I led lines of kids to special education. Okay, so I wasn't actually asked to lead the line of kids to special education and, in fact, didn't even know how to get there. As I walked behind the teacher through the playground breezeways, I fantasized that I was the second in command and could take over at a moment's notice should the teacher suddenly be hit by an off-course ball, which is virtually the same as actually leading the line. I felt that this experience had prepared me for my new role, and I was anxious to take my classmates wherever they needed to go.

Being viewed as a helper in class took the sting out of being called retard and other not-so-attractive names like booger-head, but let's face it, I still couldn't read or spell my way out of a wet paper bag. While my mom would have been cheering, "Way to bang those erasers, honey!" other people might have had another view, such as, "She can bang an eraser, but she still can't learn!" Something has to be said, though, for the effort my teacher was making to help me view myself differently because I was making progress, and even my peers began to view me differently. If this is all I got from Miss Derek, her investment would have been well-placed, because I believe half the battle in education, maybe more than half, is self-esteem.

Who knew when I would learn to read and when my writing wouldn't look like chicken scratches? Miss Derek concentrated on things like staying in my seat without irritating everyone, learning to pay attention and actually be attentive, and being out of my seat only if I had a purpose. These were important objectives. They may not seem academic, but they have everything to do with a child's success at school. Furthermore, her belief in me—evidenced by giving me responsibilities—made me want to go to school, always a good thing. My philosophy is if the kid is in your class and breathing, there is a chance to reach that kid. No doubt Miss Derek subscribed to this view.

For someone without a master's degree in special education, Miss Derek sure did know a lot about working with me. Some of it was common sense, I guess, but I believe she was also naturally gifted and blessed with a heart for kids. I know there were times when she must have been so frustrated with me. I still was prone to be very impulsive. I once got into a fight with a boy who tried to come into our class at recess. I was inside the classroom because I was sick. I was put in charge while Miss Derek went to the office to pick up handouts. I took my job seriously. This overzealous child who shall remain anonymous (Billy Spundoc) attempted to come into the classroom before the bell rang. I jumped at the chance to lay down the law and began pulling against the door with all my might. One of us pulled too hard and then let go, and both of us fell on the floor. With the doorknob nearly broken and both of us on the floor, Miss Derek arrived on the scene none-too-pleased. I felt like such a jerk. I knew that when she said I was in charge, she didn't mean "break the door." It's just one of the many times I wished I wasn't so random.

Miss Derek had an unusually tight grip on my arm as she dragged—I mean, led—me to the office where my mom was waiting to take me to a doctor's appointment. Miss Derek lectured me all the way to the office, likely venting her bottled-up frustration from previous incidents when she had shown more restraint. The short walk down the hall seemed to take forever. When we arrived, she tried to soften the pained expression on her face as she greeted my mom. Mom needed no explanation. She knew I had done something wrong but waited until we got to the car before she began her lecture. I promised to think about what I was doing next time and vowed to stay out of trouble. We both knew it would just be a matter of time before I fell off the wagon. The next day Miss Derek tried to pretend that what would thereafter be called "the door incident of 1973" never happened. Thankfully, she was a good actress. I couldn't forget, though. I think I liked it better when I didn't know why someone was mad!

NOWHERE TO GO BUT UP

As summer vacation approached, I prepared to leave Miss Derek's class, but I did so with mixed feelings. Yes, I was grateful to be out of school, but I would miss her. She had become an unlikely friend. Many of my little "misfit" buddies had either moved away or were in full-time special education. Miss Derek seemed to get me as much as anyone ever got me. With not a single one of my peers to really call a friend, I looked to her as a source of support. Though she could be stern with me, I knew she cared. I wasn't sure if anyone would ever want to have me in class as she had, especially if I couldn't read. Even if I could clean desks and sweep floors. I was pretty sure those talents weren't going to be enough to keep me in public school for another year. I was not sure what was going to happen to me.

I had heard of kids who had been held back. That to me seemed a terrible fate. As much as I had come to look forward to Miss Derek's class, I didn't want to repeat a grade. At the rate I was going, I was sure I'd be in second grade until I was 40. My mom was aware that when you don't know how to read when exiting second grade, the options for third grade would include retention or an institution. I was living on borrowed time. No one in the administration of my school thought I could learn. Miss Derek had done her best, but I still couldn't read. With that in mind, retention seemed likely. My mom feared the worst.

5

Another Chance

I felt destined to be held back, but a few gains in reading and my teacher's willingness to be creative in her assessment of my progress gave me a chance to move forward.

Who would have guessed that Miss Derek (knowing no other teacher would take me and that I could be institutionalized) would aspire to become a third-grade teacher and express a desire to have Shari Rusch (the child no one else would dare claim) in her class for the second year in a row? While others may have questioned her sanity, my mother viewed her "career move" as a modern-day miracle. I was being given another chance.

As I took my seat at the front of the class (a place chosen with great care for me by Miss Derek) I hoped, as always, that this year would be different.

B AND D AND OTHER MYSTERIES

One of the mysteries of life to me was why a letter (a blob of ink on a page) such as "d" was a "d". I also was confounded by why a letter such as "d" made a "du" sound. What I couldn't explain, I just had to accept, which meant I had to accept a lot. Once I started accepting that certain things were true (S-H-A-R-I spelled my name), I was able to memorize facts. Nothing was on an analytical or higher level. I couldn't explain to you *why* something was; I just had to learn to say "It is!"

I wrestled with the shape, meaning, and sound of letters until I couldn't wrestle anymore. That was the day that "d" became a "d" and an "l" became an "l." Actually sometimes an "I" was "L" and "F" was an "E", but let's not get picky.

Accepting that a letter was, well, what it *was* didn't change the fact that I had dyslexia—a word I refused to let people say out loud in my presence, because I thought if they didn't say it, then I wouldn't have it. Well, I had "it" all right. As a result of "it," my eyes told my brain all kinds of goofy things and caused me untold difficulty with reading and writing.

On many days literally every letter of the alphabet would frustrate me. "These stupid letters that move around on the page, reversing themselves and disappearing; they make me so confused. Why do they reverse themselves?" I would mutter to myself. "Why do they move? Why can I recognize 'W' one day and the next day I can't?" I would ask out loud. No answers were coming.

As I laid my body on a book and tried to keep the words

from running off the page, I felt defeated. One strange detail: the brighter the light in the room, the more the words moved, disappeared, and reversed themselves. Sadly, I was not allowed to turn off the lights and place everyone in the dark simply because dim or no light worked better for me. Go figure. It would be years before anyone even acknowledged that my choice to operate in dim or no light wasn't just a personality quirk, but a response to a learning problem.

Don't get me started on my writing; that's a whole other story for sure. Oh, the many days I would approach this task with dread. My hand would become so fatigued due to my effort to get control of the small muscles in my hand that I experienced intense physical pain. I knew what I wanted to do, but the muscles in my hand would not take direction from my head. So I would grip the pencil tighter and try to strong-arm it into doing the right thing. The truth is, even if my hand would take direction, my brain was not giving it accurate information. There were many times that I looked up at the board or a book, attempted to copy something, and the signal sent from my head to my hand seemed to be distorted. The result of this distortion was strangely shaped letters, reversals, and in some cases, unrecognizable words, blobs, and smears of pencil lead.

Even on the days I actually wrote something that resembled letters, my "brain/hand problem" resulted in a very inconsistent writing style. Sometimes my hand got so tired, I would resort to a clumsy form of writing, big and loopy. Without control over my pencil, I would use most of a piece of paper to write my name. The next day, or even the next hour, I would write everything extremely small as I held the pencil tight and tried to control my hand. Staying within the lines was difficult, requiring deep concentration and intense pressure on my pencil to maintain control. Often my grip was so tight, my hand would shake. My writing papers often had holes in them or accordion tears. The pressure I put on my pencil was so intense, I often left my paper damaged because I wrote too hard.

Miss Derek was very diplomatic when looking at my papers. I am sure she had to suspend her natural inclination to play teacher and offer "constructive criticism." Her critiques would have never ended if she had taken this route. Instead, she opted for a different approach. When looking at a paper with holes of several dimensions, and letters and words that few could decipher, she would attempt to find the good. A single stroke of my pencil that wasn't too dark, or a shape even remotely resembling a letter, would receive praise.

As you may have noticed, I have hardly mentioned numbers. It is because most of my early years were spent feeling that all numbers—particularly 3, 5, 7, and 9—were in a conspiracy against me. At some level I believed these numbers were, in fact, evil and might take over the world. Or, at the very least, they were working in a sinister way to make me fail arithmetic.

When it comes to numbers, all of my "I don't get it" rules apply here: reversals, omissions, tracking problems; literally anything that occurred with letters related to reading and writing also happened with numbers. If the light was too bright, and I ate Cheerios for breakfast (I ate Cheerios every day), 3 would surely turn into an E and 5 was an S. Did I mention that 6 and 9 looked the same to me and were practically interchangeable? On a good day I could do some basic addition and subtraction. The problem was, there weren't many good days. I would look at a page with 3 + 3 and see 5 + 5. I would painstakingly count each one of my fingers several times to ensure that 5 + 5 was 10. This was a slow process, by the way, because I wasn't that swift at counting. I would often get distracted while counting, and I would count some of the same fingers over again. When you count your own fingers and you get 12, it can cause some serious anxiety.

When did I grow two fingers? I wondered. When I finally determined that 5 + 5 was 10, and that I had not grown two fingers, I carefully wrote 3 + 3 = 10.

REFUELING: OTHERWISE KNOWN AS 100 WAYS TO GET OUT OF YOUR SEAT

I was always so proud of my work—because I rarely finished anything. When I did finish something, even if it was just one problem, I was bursting at the seams with excitement. Never one to keep anything to myself, especially my hands and voice, I would often attempt to share every step of progress with those around me. Miss Derek eventually was able to direct me away from distracting my peers by allowing me to come to her desk for encouragement. Once again I ask, *What was she thinking?* The poor woman could never get anything done, because I was always glued to her side ready to tell her the (tedious and boring—I mean, thrilling) story of how I had learned that four apples take away one apple was two apples. With great patience

Miss Derek would explain that four apples take away one apple is actually three, but she was quick to point out how much she appreciated my effort. Satisfied that I had the wrong answer, but that Miss Derek liked me, I'd go back to my seat, and within minutes promptly return to my teacher's desk celebrating the fact that six plus two equals seven.

My third-grade teacher was ahead of her time. Now when kids get out of their seats during a lesson to get praise or reinforcement or even a drink of water, we have a 10-dollar word for this: We call it "refueling." In the past kids with learning or attention issues who left their seats constantly were just called "irritating" and "disruptive," but now we know the reason for this behavior. These children are likely exhibiting impulsiveness and probably seem a little random, but they are actually attempting to fill a need. Their bodies are filled with energy, or they may feel numbness due to internal issues such as ADHD. Their minds feel fuzzy or out of focus, and in some cases they are not operating as they should due to learning disabilities. To counteract these feelings kids will often look around, appear distracted, or even exhibit behavior problems. It is as if the internal feeling of being out of control spills out around them. When addressing these issues educators have learned that staying seated isn't always the best solution. If forced to stay seated with no hope of a break, a child's negative behaviors may arise. The answer? Allow kids to move and positively "refuel."

The need to replenish, refuel, and refocus can be dealt with as a game. Complete a task—even one small task—correctly, then honor that accomplishment with a break. Accompanied by praise, this chance to get a drink of water or stand for a minute is a great motivator. Going to the teacher's desk to "touch base," ask a question, and get praise or direction on the work allows a child another means of refueling and refocusing. In addition to fulfilling the need to move, much-needed reinforcement from the teacher powerfully helps a kid—prone to frustration due to internal noise and learning roadblocks—to continue trudging through a challenging task. This refueling behavior obviously has to be tempered. A kid like me would stand up 20 times while reading one sentence to get some type of praise if it were allowed, but without question some opportunity for refueling was effective for me.

WORKBOOKS AND OTHER THINGS THAT WON'T CURE LEARNING DISABILITIES

On many occasions people have asked my mom what she did to help me at home during this precarious time of slow progress in school. With bated breath they wait for the answer, sure that my mom worked with me for hours on end developing a scientific method of higher-level learning strategies that would make Einstein proud. Unfortunately, there is no lofty answer my mom can offer. She was a working mom. Our lives were busy and my parents' workload was significant. My mom was facing a critical shortage of time, energy, and ideas when it came to me. While truly grateful for my placement with Miss Derek, she felt power-less to help me academically. My mom continued to make me awards for a variety of accomplishments, such as showing up for breakfast with matching socks, but life was running fast. With two parents working, there was little time to analyze my situation or know what to do to help me.

It isn't that my mom didn't try to help me learn. Oh, the many times she attempted to help me understand simple concepts such as adding two plus two. She was as bewildered as anyone by my inability to understand basic concepts. She could explain why two plus two was four all day and still get nothing but a blank look to show for it. Even she who had struggled in school was able to read and write, so my inadequacies baffled her.

At one point Mom enlisted my sister's help. Surely Shawn, the "Golden Child" (the girl I would point out to complete strangers, saying, "Did you know my sister can sit quietly?") could explain to me why two plus two was four or why the word Bob was spelled "bob" not "dod." Shawn entered this task with great enthusiasm, sure that those who came before were slightly inept. She lasted about five minutes, then proclaimed with exasperation that I needed to stop goofing around and pay attention. She stormed from the room and took her pencil box with her. My dad was probably as confused by my problems as everyone else in our family. Thankfully for him, he had to work long hours, or he would have found himself across the table from me thoughtfully attempting to explain that it wasn't "dog" who so loved the world, it was God.

Initially my mom's response to every failing grade in school was to take me to the local drugstore and buy me a workbook. I still remember the shelf, which seemed a mile high and overflowed with paperback books full of activities designed to teach me something. My mom and I made this trip many times. We would bring the new workbook home with great expectations. After cracking the spine, everyone in the family took a turn at explaining information from the first page. When we were all sufficiently frustrated with the book and each other, it landed on a shelf with all the other workbooks that came before and collected dust.

While it was clear that academic pursuits would continue to be, at the very least, challenging, my ever-optimistic mother was not about to give up. Though I was Miss Derek's favorite pupil (according only to me), being called "retard" made my self-esteem hover somewhere below zero. Mom clung to the hope that if she found an outlet for me that was "mainstream" (not that head-running wasn't), I would get much-needed praise and at least blossom into a resistant reader with a hobby.

Ah, you ask yourself, "What kind of outlet would be good for a kid like her?" Let's just say up front that sports were not a viable option because my family feared I would die at the hands of a soccer ball (as near-death experiences during soak 'em and square ball had proved). I couldn't read words; therefore, it was assumed I wouldn't be able to read music (a safe bet), so an instrument was out. As for art, I found it difficult to hold scissors, let alone use them, so my mom moved to the obvious. She decided to take my experience as a singer (I actually didn't have any) to the next level.

My mom was pretty clear about the fact that few talent agents would be looking for a lisper with lazy-eye blindness, so she decided to take matters into her own hands. As her modeling agency grew, she was asked to do a variety of fashion shows and special events where her models were featured. While I was reluctant, she convinced me that her fashion shows would not be successful without a seven-year-old to sing at some point during each show. While some on the outside might have wondered why I needed to sing "Somewhere Over the Rainbow" in the middle of a fashion show for a local department store, my mom justified it somehow, and I became "half-time" entertainment.

People seemed to like the kid who sang, even if she had a lisp that obscured some words. Applause erupted and the word "cute" was often used. Since I was sure they were speaking about someone else, no one ever had to fear my getting a big head.

DO YOU KNOW THE WAY TO SAN JOES?

While I was busy becoming a star after school and on weekends, reality continued at school. I plodded through assignments, crossing my fingers all the way. I was not consistent about anything except my inconsistency. Constantly battling my environment (hot/cold, light/dark, noise/quiet) and internal issues (energy, allergies, impulsiveness, dyslexia) made every day a dizzying experience of contradictions. Always moving a little forward then a little back, I found my frustration with school never ceased. "I am paying attention, but still don't understand. My clothes irritate my skin, making me so distracted I can't pay attention. It is too bright in here, so the words on my page are running around. My nose is running because I dared drink milk yesterday, and now I can't think because I don't feel well." It was like swatting a massive swarm of flies while trying to learn.

Even amid these distractions, I was seeking to please. Miss Derek was my hero, so I was trying not to let her down. While I was good at excuses, my teacher kept me on my toes, expecting me to keep up with the "normal" kids. I was comfortable with this arrangement. I would offer an excuse, she would push me forward, and sometimes I even got the work done on time and did it right. She would sometimes make accommodations for me by shortening assignments so I could keep up.

Then a bomb, known as the states and capitals, dropped. I was not aware at the time that there were 50 states and each one had a capital. I was blissfully happy not knowing this information. I knew that I lived in the United States and all; I just didn't realize there were so many states. As Miss Derek described it, our assignment was to learn all the states and capitals and their locations on a map. Upon hearing this my mouth fell wide open, I began drooling, and my eyes rolled back in my head. *Excuse me? * I said in my head. *She can't be serious. * I was pretty sure Miss Derek was putting something interesting into her teacup. After I closed my mouth and adjusted my eyes, I came to my senses. *That Miss Derek, she is clever. Surely she doesn't expect me to learn all of the states and capitals. I bet she has another assignment for me.*

I was shocked and saddened to learn that for this assignment, Miss Derek did not plan to make an accommodation for me. There would be no shortening of the assignment here. *That's it! * I thought. *She is officially off my birthday party list! * I went to her desk, hoping to talk some sense into her. She wouldn't budge. I offered to learn where 10 very important states were. She shook her head in disagreement. "Okay, I will learn 20. Let's make it 20," I said, as though I were an auctioneer. This suggestion was once again met with a negative head-shake. *Ooh! She is being so unreasonable,* I thought. How was I supposed to learn the location of 50 states and 50 capitals? According to my math this was something like 150 locations!

I felt totally defeated. As I walked home, a somber death march played in my head. My life as I knew it was over. Even my mom, though trying to hide it, was shocked. She stuttered and sounded frightened when she said, "You have to do what?" I knew if my mom was scared, I should go hide my head right now. She was the optimist, and I saw a noticeable tremor in her hands. Again trying to hide her fear, she said, "I know, we'll go get a workbook." I started crying.

I love you, Mom, I thought, *but no workbook is going to solve this problem.*

My mom reached down and put her hand on my shoulder. "Don't worry," she said. "We'll figure it out."

"Figuring it out" meant spending days in our back room with a puzzle. The back room and the puzzle were my mom's idea, by the way. Mom knew I needed quiet—something I hated but knew was needed for this task. Our back room was the quietest place in our house. You had to walk through my sister's room to get there, and it didn't offer much to distract me. The puzzle was also my mom's idea. She knew I often had to move while learning and suggested I should remove a piece and say the state and capital out loud. Though every fiber in my body said run, stare out a window, do anything but this, I had a score to settle. Miss Derek had dared me to learn the states and capitals, and though I thought she might have gone crazy, I was going to try.

My effort at first wasn't very fruitful. I tried to memorize everything at once. My mom realized I was failing and suggested I concentrate on only three or four states at a time, breaking up the whole map into parts. Sounds a lot like the way I learned to make a bed, doesn't it? I figured out that, even in small increments, learning the states and capitals was brutally slow and not very productive unless I added a trick. I called this trick "taking pictures" when I later described it to my mom. I would take a piece of the puzzle out of the board and hold it in my hand. I looked at the puzzle and attempted to memorize the two words (state and capital) on the piece. I said the words out loud several times. I then closed my eyes and tried to see the puzzle piece in my head and its location on the map. If I couldn't close my eyes and see it, I knew I didn't have it, so I would start the process over.

Each day after school I would run around my head or run around the house and get my energy out, then trudge to the back room. Battling my desire to do anything but this, I began another "picture taking" session. The weird thing is, sometimes the pictures I had taken the day before would be gone like the wind, nowhere to be found. I spent a lot of time learning new states and capitals and just as much time relearning the ones I had learned the day before. The good news is that relearning took less time. Some fragment of the information stayed in my head, which made the process less challenging.

When the day of the test came, I was miserable. The fear was unbearable. I had only felt that nauseous once before, when I got food poisoning from barbecued pork I ate on an airplane.

I got to school hoping and praying my brain wouldn't fly out a window but fairly certain it might. I don't know what we did the whole day. Nothing else mattered. I was totally distracted by the test. I kept closing my eyes and seeing a rush of capitals and states like a snowstorm in my mind. It wasn't looking good for the home team. My nerves were too strong. I felt hot tears brimming in my eyes but tried to hold them back, so the kids in my class wouldn't see.

When the test was finally placed in front of me, a wave of anxiety overcame me. I got a prickly feeling like a thousand ants running all over my body. My brain was completely out of focus, and I wished I could disappear. I stared at the map. If only staring were an effective way to take a test. It seemed hopeless. I was drawing a blank. After hours of dealing with puzzle pieces in our back room, that map should have looked vaguely familiar. It didn't. Well, okay, the *outline* of the map looked familiar, but the *inside* of the map was making me feel queasy.

I began rocking in my chair, a familiar movement that often helped me get to sleep at night. While sleeping wasn't what I was shooting for, I needed something to calm myself. I was out of control. Miss Derek pretended not to notice, but she must have known I was in trouble. She came over, put her hand on my shoulder, and suggested I get started. Once again I felt tears in my eyes and tried to fight them back. What to do? What to do? I closed my eyes and begged God for help.

"One state one capital," I pleaded silently. Though I was in the midst of a crisis necessitating the need to close my eyes, it was actually an answer to my desperate prayer. When I closed my eyes and began pleading, I felt transported to the back room of our house. With my eyes still closed, I pictured myself with my puzzle in front of me. I could see myself pick up the Washington State puzzle piece. I shut my eyes tighter and scrunched my forehead, as if that would help me remember the words written on the puzzle piece. Washington is all that came to mind, so I scrunched my forehead even more. It seemed as if an eternity passed, then there it was. I could see it! I could hear myself speak. *Olympia!* the voice in my head shouted. I jumped in my chair, startled that I could see the picture, stunned that I remembered the name.

With great fervor and excitement I wrote "Worshigten, Olempiu" in the space allotted. Oops! At no time in our history has Washington been spelled Worshigten. In my efforts to learn the states and capitals, no one had suggested I learn how to spell them too.

Now on a roll, I kept closing my eyes and seeing the states. I just didn't see them spelled correctly. After tensing my body and closing my eyes, I would furiously write "Nert Docota." *Victory!* I would say to myself. I was feeling invincible as I wrote "Kaleforna, Sacrimneto."

I was the last one to finish the test; I even stayed in at recess to finish it. I desperately wanted to go out on the playground, but my personal vendetta against the states and capitals was being carried out and had to be completed. I wrote "Rode Iland" with a defiant sweep of my thick elementary school pencil, as if I were wielding a sword against an evil foe. I felt sure I had beaten the states and capitals at their own game. Soon Miss Derek would see that even the kid who can't tell the difference between a d and a b can figure out where "Misori" is!

I went home and told my mom, "I aced the test." I didn't know what aced meant, but I had heard someone say it before in relation to doing well on a test and decided to try it out. Aced sounded good when I said it! Way better than "flunked." I decided to use the word as often as possible.

I walked a little taller for the next couple of days. I felt smug, knowing I had "aced" the test. With eager anticipation, I looked forward to getting it back with a perfect grade at the top. It seemed Miss Derek gave the tests back to everyone but me. I was sure she was saving the best for last. When she finally laid my paper to rest on my desk, imagine my shock when I saw red all over it. In Miss Derek's class, red was not a Christmas color; it was the sign of trouble. I was all too familiar with the color red and was none too happy to see it. At the top of my test, also in red of course, it said, "50%." *Hmmm, what does that mean?* I wondered.

I ran up to the teacher's desk and said, "What does this 50 mean?" She said in soft tones, trying to be delicate, "Shari, you got a few spellings of the states and capitals right, but most of them were spelled wrong. Here is the good news, though." She tried to point out the bright side of the situation. "You got most of the locations right. Okay, so you reversed Idaho and Iowa as well as Montana and Minnesota, but other than that, you got most of them right."

"So you're saying I got half the test right?" I asked for clarification.

"Yes, half," she said, trying to sound positive.

I think I might have rolled my eyes at this point. My legs were unsteady. Miss Derek put her hand on my shoulder and said, "I'm proud of you! Don't be discouraged."

I went back to my desk, slumped in my chair, and crushed my paper, my dumb 50-percent, red-inked paper, into my desk. When I came home that day, I didn't tell my mom I got my test back. It would be several days before she found the wrinkled paper in my backpack.

After finding the paper she took me aside and tried to be encouraging. "Your puzzle method worked," she said. "You learned where most of the states were. Well, except for Iowa, Idaho, Minnesota, and Montana, but who cares about those states?" She was trying to be positive.

I was guessing the people who lived in those states cared, but I didn't say anything. Trying hard to sound upbeat she said, "You learned where most of the states are, and that is what matters. So you didn't learn how to spell them . . ." she halted. She was about to say that spelling didn't matter but knew it actually did. Her voice trailed off, then she said, "Let's go get a workbook."

Aw, the old workbook trick. She and I both knew a workbook wasn't going to help me spell, but we got one anyway. It was our ritual when things went wrong. It didn't make me feel better, but it seemed to make my mom feel better, so I went with it.

While the states and capitals test didn't completely defeat

me, it certainly left a mark. My impression was, *No matter how hard I try, I am probably going to fail.* While this was not completely true, it felt true.

Just when I thought "not trying" was a good idea, Miss Derek entered the room carrying a bunch of boxes filled with the most unlikely way for me to succeed—taking my mind completely off of Missouri (or was it Montana?).

A Sophomore-level Word for "New Reading Program"

Miss Derek seemed to be especially excited that day, as she was summoned to the classroom door by someone from the office. When the door opened, everyone in our classroom glimpsed a pallet of boxes in the hallway outside. Suddenly, chatter erupted among the students. *What could it be?* everyone wondered. Miss Derek turned in the doorway and put her finger to her lips indicating we needed to be quiet. But it was hard to contain our excitement. A delivery of boxes was not an everyday occurrence.

The pallet was too heavy to carry in one trip from the hallway, so Miss Derek enlisted volunteers. Unable to escape my hand waving wildly in her face, she could hardly avoid asking me to help. I hoped these special boxes contained toys or games, and I eagerly offered my volunteer services so I might be the first to see what was harbored inside. You could feel excitement in the air because something special was going to happen. It was that feeling of looking forward to a present from a loved one on

Christmas when you hurriedly, and with great excitement, unwrap the package expecting a much-anticipated toy. Now cut to the part where you open the package and find not a toy, but a hand-crocheted set of yellow earmuffs.

Once the boxes were unwrapped, the excitement drained out of me. *What?* I thought as I opened the first box. *How can it be?* Inside the boxes were what seemed to be hundreds of books. I was so disappointed. They might as well have been yellow earmuffs.

Miss Derek lifted the first box in her hands and with great enthusiasm proclaimed, "Children, this is our new reading program." There was a big silence as everyone processed this news, each determining how to react. Miss Derek smiled and nodded, as if to indicate this would be a good time for applause. The kids began to clap and cheer. Miss Derek looked elated and totally satisfied that her students understood the magnitude of this announcement.

While the other kids cheered, I sat on the floor amid boxes and brown wrapping paper, trying to get a grip. *A new reading program? I don't even know how to use the old reading program. Great, just great.*

I was having a hard time listening as Miss Derek discussed the virtues of this new program, but she continued anyway. "You will choose books from our in-class library, and when you are finished with the book, you will take a test to determine your comprehension of what you read." *Comprehension* was a huge word. I didn't know what it meant but was fairly sure I wasn't good at it.

I am guessing most of the kids in our class didn't know what comprehension meant either, but they pretended to be excited. I, on the other hand, couldn't hide my disappointment.

"When you finish all of the books in box one," she continued, "you can move on to the books in the next box."

I was grumbling, "What fun!" under my breath.

Miss Derek seemed sure that everyone understood the program and began cleaning up the remnants of packaging. Several helpers took the brightly colored boxes of books to tables set up in the back of the room. I helped Miss Derek clean up the paper and discarded boxes from the floor as everyone else ran over to see the new books. When I was done, I went back to my seat and looked out the window.

Miss Derek must have sensed I was troubled. She came over to my desk and took my hand, leading me back to the boxes filled with books. Gently moving some of the children aside to make room for me, she chose a book from a box labeled "One." I eventually learned that the books were labeled so the numbers got higher as the difficulty increased. She handed me a book with an animal on the front of it. I liked the picture and decided to open the book. Inside were more pictures. *Just my style,* I thought. I fingered through each page, looking only at the pictures and trying to pretend there weren't any words on the pages. The book was new and pretty with a soft cover that was easy to hold. Miss Derek asked if I'd like to take the book to my desk for a little while. I nodded and returned to my desk to look through the book again.

Slowly, each child returned to his or her desk with a book.

Most children had books from the Level One box as Miss Derek directed most students to start there. Everyone was given a few minutes to look through the books. In that short time some kids actually read theirs.

While looking at the pretty pictures on each page of my book, my concern about this program grew. There were maybe 10 or 20 boxes of books in the library. I guessed that not all of those books were filled with pictures. I wasn't sure if I could read the first book, let alone all the books in the library. Then Miss Derek held out a carrot that changed my attitude. "If anyone in this class finishes all of the books in the library," she said, "I will have lunch with you."

The class grew quiet, then everyone said, "Ohhhhh," in unison. This was huge. Everyone knew it. While eating with the teacher was considered a privilege, I had more than my share of this opportunity. You see, kids like me often get to eat lunch with the teacher because no one else will sit with us, or because we are in trouble. As much as I appreciated Miss Derek's willingness to be my lunch buddy, I had hoped one day she would have lunch with me for a good reason, not because she had to. This was my chance. Furthermore, I was intrigued with the idea of actually seeing Miss Derek eat. I knew she did eat, but because I had never actually witnessed it, I was left with a bit of skepticism.

Teachers usually worked while students ate. When recess came, they would lock their classroom doors and escape with Tupperware and brown bags into a mysterious place called the Teachers' Lounge. There was a lot of intrigue associated with this place, as only a precious few children had ever been given entrance—those office helpers and other special kids who were trusted with the top-secret activities that went on behind the lime-green door near the school kitchen.

While there were no promises, the mere suggestion that I might gain entrance to the teachers' lounge—and maybe, just maybe, see Miss Derek bite into a tuna fish sandwich—was all the motivation I needed to determine I would conquer the new reading program.

With fear, trepidation, and a bit of loathing for the written word, I stared at the first sentence below the pictures in my Level One book. I dared myself to try just one word, all the while keeping the vision of Miss Derek and her tuna sandwich fresh in my mind. Surely one word would look familiar. The words danced around and reversed themselves. There were only three on the bottom of the page, but they were moving so much, it looked like 10. I rummaged through my desk and grabbed two rulers, placing one under the three-word sentence and another above it. I felt somewhat victorious as the words floated between the two lines. "You can't run around now," I whispered to myself. I quickly realized I needed to put a pencil on the end of the rulers to keep the words from running off the page from between the two rulers.

Once again I stared at the words, willing my mind to recognize the three-word sentence: The rabbit hops. This wasn't rocket science, but my brain would not give me a break. I looked away and shook my head, as if moving the contents of my brain around inside my skull would initiate some kind of recognition. Nothing. Miss Derek saw me fidgeting and shaking my head.

Not an unusual sight I might add, but one that deserved attention. I was stuck and she knew it. As if to suggest that everyone was shaking the contents of their brains to recognize a word, she said to the whole class, "If you get stuck on a word, try to sound it out." What a novel idea. I knew I was supposed to sound it out, but I couldn't remember the sounds.

"What to do, what to do?" I whispered.

I immediately decided to give up on the word "the." This was one of those tricky words that didn't "sound out" easily, and I knew it. No sense in wasting time on it. I decided to attempt sounding out the word "hop." With a halting speech pattern resembling someone choking, I spoke the sounds, "hhhhhhhhh ooooooo ppppppp." It came out sounding like the word "hope" drawn out too far, but at least I was in the ballpark. "Hope," I said as if to confirm it to myself. After much frustration I asked Miss Derek to help me with the other two words and learned the rest of the sentence was: The rabbit. *Great!* I thought. *Now I can read the whole sentence: The rabbit hope.*

Wait a minute, I thought, *The rabbit hope? What does that mean?* There was no time to try to figure out the author's meaning; I had a hundred books to read. With no clear picture of why a rabbit would hope, I moved on to the next page just in time to be stymied by the sentence: The rabbit hops. Same words but they looked brand-new.

When you read a sentence wrong and think that rabbits are hoping, but you're not sure what they're hoping for, multiple problems occur when you try to read and answer the questions on a comprehension test:

What does the rabbit like to do? (a) hop (b) stop (c) pop
(d) hope

After much frustration with my attempts to read the question, Miss Derek read it to me. I returned to my desk and seriously thought I was a genius! "Of course, rabbits like to hope!" I said out loud. Doesn't everyone know that? It is so obvious." I circled the (d) with too much energy and ripped a hole in the test paper.

Sure I got all the answers right, I went to Miss Derek's desk to deliver my slightly damaged comprehension test. Still unsure of what comprehension was, but feeling more confident I might have it, Miss Derek looked over my answers. Her face got a little scrunchy and concerned, but then she took a deep breath and said, "Shari, what an excellent job you have done. You read your first book and took the test. (Notice she didn't say I got the answers right on the test.) I was overwhelmed with pride. Leaving hopeful rabbits behind, I ran to the back of the class and got another Level One book. I eagerly opened the book to learn: "The flower is petty (pretty)." I had often suspected that flowers were petty but now it was confirmed.

Miss Derek, heartened by my enthusiasm, encouraged me to ask for help often in sounding out words, so I wouldn't mistakenly think that flowers were petty or rabbits hope. She never gave the slightest suggestion that my efforts were in vain. She wasn't offering letter grades on my comprehension tests though; she just reviewed them offering verbal comments. Her praise fueled me onward from one book to the next, undeterred by sentences such as: "The boy is sab (sad)." I had no idea what "sab" was, but I wasn't going to let that stop me from reading the next book.

Though I struggled, some exciting things were happening. More and more "sight" words that you should recognize right away were becoming automatic. The word *the* was no longer my nemesis and simple words like *and, but,* and *or* no longer made me draw a blank. With rulers in hand I corralled the words on each page, getting all the easy words right and, when necessary, inventing the meaning of sentences that contained words I couldn't recognize or sound out. If Miss Derek wasn't busy, she would help me sound out words and even gave me words I was having trouble with. Those were the best stories, the ones she helped with, because they actually made sense.

As the year progressed Miss Derek saw my reading skills blossom. I went from a non- or limited reader to being a reader. Again, there were some pitfalls. Not remembering what I read could be considered a pitfall. Oh, and the part about not comprehending what I read could be considered a pitfall. But Miss Derek didn't let these little problems get in the way of her enthusiasm for my progress. Mainly concerned with getting me reading—even if my progress was on the lower end of the scale—she held out hope that comprehension and retention would improve in time. If she wanted to know what I read, she would ask me right away and was willing to accept an inaccurate, albeit interesting, summary of the story.

While hard to believe, it is an undisputed fact that I was the first and only person in our classroom to finish the new reading program. Other kids worked on the program sporadically; I spent all my time on it. Miss Derek would stop me periodically to have me pay attention during other lessons, but she gave me virtually uninterrupted access to the library in the back of class. In return for my effort, at the end of the year I was allowed to eat lunch with Miss Derek at her desk. While I was disappointed not to eat our special lunch in the teachers' lounge, I did discover the mystery food that sustained Miss Derek. I would tell you what this top secret delicacy is, but then you would have to kill me.

Always with a method to the madness, Miss Derek knew that for me to go on to the fourth grade, I'd not only have to be able to read but have to demonstrate I'd accomplished certain objectives. No doubt she had to fudge (in a Christian way) my progress in many subjects to get me to the point of passing, but it was a fact heralded throughout the class and to the administration that I had finished the new reading program.

At the end of the year Miss Derek reported to my mother that I was well above grade level in reading. For some reason Mom came home from her discussion with my teacher sure that I could read high-school-level words. I mean really higher, like sophomore level. I am fairly sure this was hopeful thinking on my mother's part, but to this day she claims this to be true. At the time I didn't know what sophomore-level meant but was glad my mom was happy.

As the end of the year approached, it became clear that— regardless of my ongoing personal issues with numbers and letters—Miss Derek was planning to promote me to fourth grade.

This was either a desperate attempt to save me from retention and/or expulsion or a clear indication that Miss Derek didn't want me in her third-grade class the next year. Even though I still believed at some level that flowers were petty and that 10 + 10 = 17, she took into consideration all things and determined that, judging from where I started, a few petty flowers were not worth holding me back.

AN END AND A BEGINNING

I left Miss Derek's class with great sadness. She had been such a leader in my life, and though I tested her patience time and again, she never gave up on me.

I knew my writing wasn't up to par, but I made her a funny little card that said something like, "tank yu." For someone who reads sophomore-level words (ha-ha) my card left a little to be desired. But ever tactful, Miss Derek took my card as if it were most precious and read it without raising an eyebrow. She then placed it in a box of presents and cards to take home, and I felt sure she might frame it.

My mom brought a cake and party favors to our classroom's end-of-the-year party. She was so grateful to Miss Derek, it was the least she could do. While our class feasted on goodies, I sat with a full plate and a heavy heart. Once again I worried about the future. I knew I was going to be in someone's class, but what would happen to me once there? I felt conflicted. I had passed to fourth grade but knew it was by a very slim margin and the flowery prose of Miss Derek. I knew I was but a breath away from a self-contained classroom or worse. I suddenly experienced a flood of memories about getting hit on the head with writing utensils. I spent the rest of our class party wondering what type of pens my new teacher might have.

6

Giant Pens and Other Night Terrors

Low self-esteem ruled me. The acceptance of my teacher was not
enough to overcome the countless examples of how I didn't fit in.
Realizing that what everyone had been saying about me for so long
was true diminished any progress I made. Longing for friends and
wishing for academic success, but believing neither was possible, I
learned to hide in the back of the class hoping to get by.

Anticipation, or should I say fear, mounted as I waited to
learn my class assignment. With anxiety heightened I had
nightmares about a toothless ogre wielding a giant pen. Just
before I was about to be plunked with a super-sized ballpoint
pen, I would wake up in a cold sweat.

I was relieved to learn my teacher was neither toothless nor
an ogre, at least not during working hours. He was actually a

nice guy with curly red hair. He was young and new at the school, two factors which I firmly believed led to my being assigned to his class. "Let's give the new guy Shari," knowing people said with sinister laughter. Apparently, I had been called "retard" too many times and was becoming paranoid. I just couldn't believe anyone would take me willingly. I could only assume he had been duped.

TALES FROM THE BACK OF THE CLASS

Though I had actually tried various ways to stop time, the first day of school came all too soon. I set foot on the pavement in front of our school and suddenly felt small. I had a strange feeling, like being swallowed.

Against my better judgment I walked in the main door of our school, down an unfamiliar hallway, and into my new fourth-grade classroom. To my surprise there was Mr. Surge, greeting everyone at the door with a handshake. What made this even more peculiar was that he was smiling. Did he not know the "don't smile on the first day" rule? Everyone knew that one. You smile and kids think they can get away with anything. Apparently, he thought he could get by because he was tall and had cool hair or something, but I was worried for his safety.

After being greeted like little ladies and gentlemen, we walked into the classroom. Accustomed to seeing our names already affixed to desks, we were confused about where to sit. Where were the name tags? Where was the seating chart that places the difficult kids (polite way of saying me) next to the kids who followed rules? Had he ever taught school before? Did he not go to the teachers' meeting where everyone shares their secrets about "certain" kids who lack self-control (polite way of saying me)? I was now even more worried for Mr. Surge. Someone needed to help him, I thought.

Having experienced the job of class monitor, I felt it was my place to step in. I walked up to Mr. Surge and said, "We don't know where to sit."

Mr. Surge chuckled and said, "How about in a chair?"

Not getting the joke, of course, and feeling Mr. Surge was not grasping the seriousness of the situation, I said again, "We don't know where to sit."

Mr. Surge chuckled again and said, "You can sit anywhere you want."

This can't be right, I thought. For many years I had not been able to choose where I wanted to sit. Seeking clarification I asked, "Are you sure you want to do this?"

Mr. Surge smiled and said, "Definitely." Suddenly, the students looked like they were in a 50-yard dash or a game of musical chairs that had spun out of control.

Chairs and desks moved all over the place as kids scrambled for the best seats. After the dust settled and everyone had found a seat, I realized I hadn't. I just stood there dumbfounded, unable to move. I guess all that freedom was confusing me. Mr. Surge put his hand on my shoulder and gave a little push toward the back of the room. I walked toward the only seat left and sat down.

Okay, first the handshake thing and then an open seating

chart? What next? Just when I thought Mr. Surge was slightly crazy, he announced that we could sit next to anyone we wanted to at lunchtime. At first I was like, "Great!" But my enthusiasm quickly vanished when I realized no one ever wanted to sit next to me at lunch. Mr. Surge looked excited, so I joined the other kids in cheering this idea. "Yea!" I said and clapped my hands. I must have done so with a serious expression that didn't match my behavior. Mr. Surge, perceptive enough to get the drift that this idea was only great if you had someone to sit with, added, "Oh, by the way, if you want to eat with me at lunch, you can." I was wondering if Mr. Surge had read my mind, but I couldn't be sure. After this last statement I hated to admit it, but Mr. Surge was making me like him.

To close his opening remarks Mr. Surge told us that if we brought music to school, he would play it during lunchtime. *When will the madness end?* I thought. I loved the idea but was scared. I felt the need to rock back and forth to gain control. Miss Derek had everything rigid and orderly, and I mean that in the nicest of ways. She made me sit up front and kept things really quiet. At home I had everything tightly wound, keeping control by making lines on the floor and doing repetitive tasks. Now I was in a room where I was sitting in the back of the class and we got to play music at lunch. What was going on here? My hands were shaking, but I tried to maintain composure.

The rest of our first day of school was spent learning about Mr. Surge's rules (or lack of them) and about this thing called "personal responsibility." Mr. Surge said "personal responsibility" a lot, as if he believed we had it. I wasn't sure what it was, but it reminded me of the word *comprehension,* so I immediately thought I didn't have it. He even said that he trusted we would do the right thing, and therefore would allow us to have a lot of freedom. At this point I was absolutely certain Mr. Surge had not read my file.

A Friend Who Knows the Times Tables: Priceless

At recess I did my typical loner things: wandering around the playground, kicking dirt, and swinging on the bars if I could find a space. All I could think about was how I was going to survive in Mr. Surge's class. The "loose walls" and personal responsibility thing had me sweating. I couldn't learn when things were noisy, and somehow I just knew he was going to let people talk during work time. The thought of it made me fuzzy-headed and exhausted. Feeling sure I would be a disappointment to my new teacher, I pondered running away. I had walked away from preschool under the guise of looking for a plastic turtle; I looked up toward the heavens hoping for a reason to escape.

Just then I tripped over a little girl sitting on a wood barrier. While I was picking myself off the ground, I mumbled, "Hi."

The little girl didn't hesitate and said, "Hi, my name is Lisa." She even sounded a bit enthusiastic. I was excited by her response but also a little concerned. I was now savvy enough socially to know that if someone said hi to me, that person either didn't know me—thus, leading to a hasty end to our short-lived friendship—or was, to put it mildly, strange. I didn't mind strange. I mean, I had a chronic cough that sounded as if I were barking and a nose that never ceased running. I wasn't exactly on the "A" list, but I wondered why anyone would want to hang around with a barking girl.

It turned out that Lisa was in my class. I just hadn't noticed her because I was a little too busy feeling overwhelmed with the whole "no seating chart/music at lunch" thing. She was really shy, something I totally couldn't relate to, but we became fast friends anyway.

I'm not sure what made Lisa like me. The rest of the kids in our class, and at our school for that matter, were completely repelled by me. No one called me retard anymore; that title was reserved for kids in special education, though I think a lot of kids wondered how I made it to fourth grade. Trust me, I didn't miss being called retard, a term I could no longer laugh off. In fact, not being called retard made me even more certain I didn't want to go back to special education, even though I needed help. Even if it might have been the best thing for me, I didn't want to go back to the unventilated wing. I now was on the lowest level of the social totem pole, but make no mistake, I was a step above the special education kids and realized the distinction.

Without meaning to, I seemed to offer endless examples of why I should be kept at arm's length from my peers. I tripped, I fell, I lacked hand-eye coordination, I spoke out of turn, I talked too much, what I said didn't make sense, and the list goes on. In an effort to fit in I would often over-laugh, overdo, and over-try, which only served to turn people away. Yet still I kept trying.

Again, I have no idea why Lisa chose to spend time with me, but I wasn't going to complain. Having a friend was way better than not having one, especially when that friend didn't have a proliferation of boogers or a distinct odor. I came to learn that Lisa not only didn't smell bad, but she held my ticket out of fourth grade.

SITTING IN THE BACK AND LEARNING NOTHING

Here is a tip: When you can't hear and see very well, you shouldn't be in the back of the room! Duh. Mr. Surge wanted to give us responsibility and opened the seating chart. I walked to the back of the class and proceeded to melt into my chair. I doodled on my Pee-Chee folder and periodically looked up to give the appearance that I knew what was going on, but I didn't have a clue.

The minute I was in the back of the class it felt like someone had cut off my air. With no filter system in place, it was like trying to get past a circus before I ever got to the teacher and the blackboard. I was distracted by the light, sound, and movement and totally overwhelmed. Unable to make a connection with what was happening in the front of the room, I just withdrew into my own world.

Even though I was overflowing with energy, I knew that the key to staying below the radar was not being conspicuous. I ran wild at recess, then made every attempt to contain myself during class. I no longer left my seat repeatedly or tried to get attention by waving my hand wildly or falling off my chair. I also didn't learn anything.

A very short time into the year I was getting really good at pretending to look normal and, oh yeah, interested. While my mind ran randomly through a series of repetitive thoughts completely unrelated to school, Mr. Surge would enthusiastically talk about some lesson. I probably heard every third word.

I was becoming good at looking like I was listening. While bouncing my knee furiously beneath the desk, I would try to keep my upper body still and make eye contact and appear attentive. Sometimes I would even nod my head and mouth the word "yes," as if to suggest that the fact I was tapping my fingers inside my desk while compulsively counting each tap was not in any way impeding my understanding of what was being said.

Sometimes during these internal wrestling matches, I would meet Mr. Surge's eyes, and he would look at me as if he suspected something. Did he know it was all I could do to sit still? Did he see me reorganizing the materials on my desk compulsively in an effort to bring order to the chaos inside me? Chances are, between whatever Miss Derek had told him and what my file revealed, Mr. Surge knew school was a struggle for me. True to my assessment of him, though, he never talked to me about being slow or called attention to me in a negative way. He tried to offer as much help as he could amid the bustle of a busy class, but to be honest, I was starting to slip away.

Slipping is when you start to feel hopeless. Slipping is when your teacher cares, but is busy. Slipping means not raising your hand because you are afraid of what will come out of your mouth. Slipping is when you think there is no chance of achieving a certain skill, so you either try to avoid it or you don't give it your full effort.

Thankfully I had entered fourth grade with some skill in reading. It wasn't like I ever picked up a book for leisure, that's for sure, but now in class I recognized some grade-level words and could read what was necessary. Remembering what I read was a whole other issue. I don't know if it was from the birth trauma or some other cause, but what I read didn't stick. While this is a problem even today, when I was younger it was a significant challenge. By the time I read five sentences, I couldn't remember what the first two were about. Some of the problem came from being a slow reader. When you read really slowly and struggle with every other word, it gets tiring and hard to keep the information in order and in context.

While my reading ability (except for comprehension and retention) and my verbal skills were getting consistently better, my spelling and writing were not. I could read a word but could not re-create it in writing. I could say what I thought (sometimes) but could not put my thoughts in order on paper. This assessment of myself was confirmed when I recently found my end-of-the-year report card from fourth grade. I was not at grade level for writing and spelling but was getting close to grade level in reading. Surprisingly (or maybe not-so-surprisingly), the very lowest grades I had were in math. By the end of fourth grade there were 67 objectives that had to be completed. I had completed 11.

To me, math was just another form of reading but more complicated. In reading, if you knew the letters and sounds, you could (eventually) hope to understand what was said on a page. Math was tricky; it kept elevating and becoming more difficult.

You didn't just have to know how to read the numbers; that would be too easy (except that I got most of them backward). There were all kinds of complicated symbols indicating particular skill sets. The more abstract the concept, the more I got lost.

TIMES WHAT?

I remember the day my teacher told us about a very important math skill we had to learn. This skill was literally our ticket out of fourth grade. "Oh, please let it be 'four apples take away three apples,' " I quietly pleaded. Emphasizing the importance of this skill Mr. Surge said again, "This math skill is something you will use for the rest of your life."

What is this monumental skill that could potentially ruin my life if I don't learn it? I thought.

Then he said it: "The times tables."

"What?" I was perturbed, and I didn't even know what perturbed meant. *The times tables,* I said in my head. This didn't sound earth shattering, but then again, I didn't know what a "times table" was.

Mr. Surge pulled down a chart that looked like a graph and began explaining something about how 2 x 3 = 6. A number of kids nodded their heads as if they knew this already. Mr. Surge went on to say that if you already knew the times tables, you could advance to division. *Wait, wait, wait a minute. I still don't know what the times tables are, so don't say words like division!* I thought. I tried to calm myself by remembering that it wasn't so long ago I didn't know how to do single-digit addition.

When I was first introduced to this crazy idea that numbers with an "x" between them meant "times," I knew I was in trouble. Elusive, confusing, and downright troublesome would be good words to describe this "skill" of multiplying numbers by each other. While everyone around me seemed to accept the premise, I was totally paralyzed by the idea that "x" means "times." What? I don't get it. An x is a letter; it doesn't mean times. Even if the x did mean times, that still didn't explain why $4 x 4 = 16$.

My teacher went rounds with me trying to get me to understand that $2 x 2$ was just two twos and that $6 x 7$ was like adding six sevens together. He was saying the words, but they were not making any sort of connection with me. One explanation after another, one trip to Mr. Surge's desk after another, and still no connection. He gave me charts and flash cards—still no recognition whatsoever.

Once I learned that you had to learn the times tables for numbers 1 through 10, but that multiplication tables 1 through 10 actually meant 100 math equations, I felt overwhelmed.

One of the biggest hurdles in this whole process was that I couldn't accept or understand that $6 x 7$ was the same as $7 x 6$. According to me these were two completely different equations. I cannot explain why this was so hard for me. It was just reversing a problem. But when you don't understand the underlying concept that multiplication is just another way of adding numbers together, but quicker, all other related concepts don't make sense. I was exasperated every time someone would point out that the reverse of a multiplication problem would give you the same answer. I would dismiss their ranting and head back to my chair, sure that these people had something funny in their Kool-Aid.

As each day passed, I crept lower and lower beneath my desk becoming convinced the times tables might, in fact, kill me. I just tried to keep my focus on lunch and recess.

One day after a serious battle had been waged against 3 *x* 3, I felt disoriented, as if the room were spinning. Nothing was making sense. I laid my head down on the table. Never one to let other kids see me cry, I put my forehead on the edge of the table, and tears hit the classroom floor. I was always halfway under my desk anyway, so no one even noticed when I bowed my shoulders and hung my head.

I had lots of reasons for my tears. I was feeling like such a failure. My understanding that I was dyslexic had now given way to the easier-to-understand explanation that I was dumb. Mr. Surge was great, but there was only so much that he could do to help me. I could read but didn't remember or understand most of what I read. Sometimes I was literally laying on a book to keep the words still. Often I used rulers, pens, or other straight edges to stop the letters from running off the pages or reversing themselves. With the exception of my name and a few other important words like "stop," I couldn't spell. My writing looked, to put it mildly, sad. Addition wasn't so bad as long as I could use my fingers and toes, but subtraction, especially when borrowing was required, made me feel very small. Then there were the times tables—my ticket out of fourth grade—and I still didn't understand what the *x* meant.

I found it hard to regain my composure. The class was going

on around me, a lesson was being taught, people were moving
and talking, and no one noticed that I had quite literally slumped
under my desk. Lisa's hand found me as I made my way under
the desk, and she pulled me back to my seat. I tried to quickly
wipe my face so other people wouldn't see that I was crying.

Lisa asked, "Why are you crying?"

The question was too big. I couldn't offer all the reasons; it
would take too long. I sat quietly.

Lisa asked, "Do you want me to help you in math?"

Suddenly, a weight lifted from my shoulders and I sat back
in my chair. I took a deep breath and wiped away the last of my
tears. I said nothing but nodded my head in agreement. She
asked what I needed help with, and once again, the question was
too big. What didn't I need help with?

I started to say "addition," then murmured part of the word
"subtraction," and finally let the words "multiplication tables"
tumble out of my mouth. I confided in Lisa that I thought I
wouldn't get out of fourth grade if I didn't learn the times tables. I
went on to whisper that I didn't even know why they were called
times tables. "I mean, what does the word 'table' have to do with
anything?" I said accusingly in a louder, more audible voice.

Lisa quietly said, "Don't worry about the times tables. I will
teach you how to do them at recess." I thought Lisa was very
smart, but her plan seemed a little shaky to me. If I couldn't
learn them sitting in a chair, how was I going to learn the times
tables while swinging around on the bars? Well, as it turns out,
going around on the bars or swinging from a tree limb while trying to learn something was the key to my understanding.

Lisa quickly made good on her promise. Every day, every recess, regardless of my attention span, she kept drilling the times tables. We did a lot of walking around the playfields, and the movement made the learning—while not easy—far more enjoyable.

I have to confess that there was not higher-level understanding here. Much as in Miss Derek's class, there were just times I had to accept facts, even if I didn't understand them and couldn't explain them. When I got to the point of acceptance, then I was able to memorize better.

I won't tell you how long it took me to learn all of the times tables from 1 through 10 (150 days, 6 hours, and 45 minutes), but it was most of the school year. Oh, and add several days to understand the concept that zero times any number is zero. Through sweat and tears Lisa had prevailed. Undaunted by my slowness, she persevered.

How Much Time Do You Have?

Having finally reached the goal, and able to recite all of the times tables through 10, I was overjoyed. I was sure this meant I was going to graduate from fourth grade. I could hardly contain myself as I ran, leaped, and jumped my way around the playground trying to find Mr. Surge. I located him on the playground discussing something with another teacher. Never known for my patience, I interrupted and with great fanfare announced, "Mr. Surge, I can do the times tables. I can do 1 through 10. I want to say them to you." He held up his finger as if to indicate I needed to wait a minute, and I shuffled from foot to foot unable to stand still.

Lisa finally caught up with me after I'd left her standing on the playground shouting something like, "I have to tell Mr. Surge!" She was beaming and hopeful that Mr. Surge would see what an accomplishment this had been.

When Mr. Surge didn't turn around quickly enough, I had to interrupt again. "Mr. Surge, Mr. Surge, I have to tell you something," I said with an impassioned voice. Finally with a slight bit of annoyance in his voice, Mr. Surge turned around and asked, "Shari, what is it?"

Without hesitation I started to recite every times table from 1 through 10.

I'm sure Mr. Surge must have thought I was going to just give him a brief demonstration, but no, I kept going and going. The bell signaled the end of recess, and I walked by his side continuing the times tables. Class was about to begin, and I continued to speak, not realizing he may not have had the time or inclination to listen to all the times tables. I never caught on to anything, so if he was signaling me that he was through listening, I simply didn't get it. I kept reciting; he politely kept listening. Everyone was seated and the class had grown quiet as I stood by Mr. Surge's side rambling on. Just as I said, "Ten times ten is one hundred," the bell rang, signaling the start of class. I stood triumphant and beaming. Mr. Surge appeared slightly overwhelmed and confused.

First of all, I had just recited 100 times problems. He might have thought I said all of them because I was proud of my accomplishment. The truth is, I couldn't say them any other way. If you wanted to hear me say the times tables, you needed some spare time, because I couldn't separate one from another. If you wanted to know 6×2 you had to listen to everything from 1×1 up to 6×2.

In time I would learn to separate the smaller pieces, but that was a long way off. At the start I failed every timed test I took, because to get one problem, I had to do all the equations that led up to it. Whew!

Usually self-conscious, I felt no discomfort as I stood in front of the class waiting for Mr. Surge's response. He didn't hesitate to give me a hug and say how proud he was. I bubbled over. His praise meant the world to me. He did look puzzled, though, when he asked how I learned the times tables. I said, "My friend Lisa taught me." Lisa looked flushed and a little embarrassed by the attention but nodded her head to confirm it was true.

Mr. Surge said, "Lisa, excellent job!"

Lisa got more flushed and looked like she might run from the room. Mr. Surge changed the subject to prevent her flight. "Good job, Shari!" he said, reinforcing what he had already said. I think that was supposed to be my cue to take my seat, but I didn't budge. I stood there basking in the glow of my achievement.

Mr. Surge looked at me to gain eye contact and gave me a nod. Catching his eyes I suddenly was transported back to the classroom and realized I was standing in front of everyone. Finally aware of my circumstances, I hurriedly shuffled to my seat.

I think some other things went on that day, but I was so busy planning to get out of fourth grade that I don't know what they were. I had some big plans for myself. I was going to solve all the world's problems with my knowledge of the times tables or, at the very least, be able to recite them one at a time.

Was It Something I Said?

Mr. Surge made an announcement toward the end of the year that was very unsettling. He was moving his family to Australia to teach in a private school. I had no idea where Australia was, but I knew it wasn't one of our states and capitals. He showed us a world map and pointed to Australia. This country was really far away, it seemed.

In the school where he would teach, the kids wore uniforms and sat in straight lines. It was all too much for me. This guy with cool hair was going to a school where everyone sat in straight lines? *What happened?* I wondered. A prickly feeling came over me, and almost immediately, my suspicion was that he was leaving because of me. I couldn't pass the timed tests. I couldn't spell. Maybe I wasn't going to pass fourth grade and he didn't have the courage to tell me. Worse yet, maybe he was afraid I would be in his class again. My mind ran wild with all kinds of reasons why Mr. Surge was leaving. He assured the class that he was looking forward to this new opportunity, but I couldn't accept his explanation. I felt very unsteady. Having been so secure in the future, suddenly I was scared.

I never told my mom I thought it was my fault that Mr. Surge was leaving. In fact, I didn't mention my concern about fifth grade either. My mom seemed distracted lately and I didn't want to add to it. I was so agitated even cleaning didn't help.

Getting to sleep at night was even more difficult. Always in bed by 9, but never asleep until at least 11, my mind wandered as my body seemed electrified. I seldom heard much outside my door, but now my hearing was sensitive. There seemed to be loud discussions between my parents and a strange sort of tension hung in the air as we ate breakfast and prepared for school. My parents appeared distant from each other, and many mornings my dad was gone before I got up. While none of this seemed highly unusual, the strain of discomfort made me even more on edge.

The few remaining school days felt endless and dizzying with uncertainty. I stopped hanging out with Lisa just because I was too embarrassed to voice my fear about the future. At recess I resumed kicking dirt and circling the playfields.

Right before school got out we learned I was going to pass. As with Miss Derek the year before, Mr. Surge must have taken creative license with describing my accomplishments and made my success with the times tables (if you can call it that) significant enough to go to fifth grade. I presume that once again the school didn't want to deal with my mom, or maybe there wasn't a teacher who would have me if I stayed in fourth grade. Whatever the case, we celebrated the good news.

On the last day of school I walked out into the bright sunshine knowing I could move on to fifth grade. What a relief! I was totally clear about what I couldn't do but was glad to have squeaked by. I was still oddly concerned with Mr. Surge's departure but was happy he had let me move to the next grade. Maybe it was a parting gift to me. Still sure I had made him leave, I hoped he would return and that I could see him again.

7

And Then There Were Three

It has often been said that nothing ever stays the same. This is never so true as when you have learning challenges. Just when you think you know something, you don't. Just when you are familiar with something, it is gone. With so much instability in my mind and school experience, I clung to my family ever so tightly. Within a very short time even things I was sure of would disintegrate, leaving me wondering if there was anything I could depend on.

When I got out of school for the summer I should have felt relief, but something was amiss, and I couldn't put my finger on it. Was I feeling unsettled because my teacher was leaving or because I was concerned about the teacher I would be assigned to in fifth grade? Who knows? The only thing I did know was that I was off balance.

Over time I had developed a rigid sense of order that now crossed the line into compulsiveness. Keeping order was my way of holding on. The more my life felt out of control, the more tightly I ordered what was around me. The dependence on order was a truly positive response to physical and developmental problems, but it grew into a rigid way of life. The slightest disruption in a schedule or small change in plans would throw me into a tailspin. The only antidote was to begin ordering everything around me.

Case in point: Typically, when my mom finished modeling classes at her agency, we would go up to our cabin to spend time during the summer, but nothing had been mentioned about when or if we were going that summer. My response was to start organizing my sock drawer furiously. My mom and dad seemed to be arguing more frequently; my response was to vacuum and re-vacuum until the lines on the carpet were so deep it looked as if I was preparing to plant crops. Even while ordering everything I could get my hands on, there was no end to my feeling that something terrible was going to happen.

One night Mom hurriedly told us that we were going rollerskating with some family friends. While my sister and I were at the roller rink, my mom learned that my dad was leaving her. When we returned from skating, my mom had obviously been crying. After whispering to our family friends she informed my sister and me that our dad was gone. There were a lot of tears shed. We all had questions for which there were no answers. I spent the night praying my dad would come home.

After six weeks my dad returned to our house to meet with

us briefly. He looked thin and tired. Arriving with no luggage it was clear right from the start that he was not going to stay.

All four of us sat on the perimeter of the living room looking extremely shaken. It was obvious no one wanted this to happen, but apparently my parents thought there was no solution for their problems. My sister and I were told that our parents were getting a divorce. I guess I shouldn't have been shocked, but I was. I came unhinged at that moment. I stayed in my chair and sobbed uncontrollably. I could have begged or pleaded, but there seemed to be no hope. The plaque in our foyer that said "The family that prays together stays together" was hanging, appropriately, crooked on the wall. What a mess.

Though my dad tried to make it clear that his leaving had nothing to do with my sister and me, I didn't believe it for a minute. I was the one always messing things up and acting unpredictably. If I had been more like my sister, I thought, he wouldn't have left. If I had been older and wiser, I might have believed differently, but I was 10 and had the self-esteem of a gnat. I was sure this whole thing was my fault.

I would like to tell you that years later we all felt my parents' divorce was the right thing and that we are all better for it. Sorry, but I can't. I am convinced that with some help my parents could have stayed together. Okay, shock treatments and an exorcism may have been required, but it is possible. One thing is sure, if my parents had stayed together, my life would have been far less complicated and I would have required far less therapy as an adult.

While there may be rare exceptions, kids are not better off

when the foundation they are standing on crumbles. To sound mature they can claim they just want their parents to be happy, whatever that means. While they might succumb to the inevitable, most kids wish their families would stay intact, as I did.

Even as weak as we might have been, we were stronger when standing together. I will forever wish my parents had hung in there for our sake. They are both good people who drove each other a little crazy, but isn't that what families are for?

We were now an unwilling part of a growing trend; we were children of divorce. I heard my parents describe their situation as amicable. I now know there is no such thing. While my parents quarreled bitterly by phone and exchanged quips in person, my sister and I wondered whose side we were supposed to be on.

We saw my dad for dinner once a week, but I felt so guilty for having driven him away that I seldom said anything.

A NEW LIFE

Our house sold and we moved to an apartment complex in a town about 10 miles away. There was a bike park nearby and my school was across the street. It looked okay on the outside, but since it was just another part of the weirdness invading my life, I refused to get settled.

My mom sold her modeling agency and began doing promotions for malls. That was a time when malls had bridal shows, home shows, and other events to draw crowds. Already familiar with malls because she had done fashion shows there, she was able to step into producing specialty events fairly easily.

Though my mom was employed, money was tight. We had food to eat, but I knew to not ask for anything, though I had holes in my socks and my shoes were too small. I wore high-water pants (knowing full well they were not in fashion) without complaint because I saw my mom's hand shake when she gave our apartment manager our rent. A luxury in our house was to take a quarter from the change jar and buy a donut at the grocery store situated just below our apartments, a treat reserved for special occasions.

With my mom working long hours, my sister and I quickly became latchkey children. Wearing keys around our necks, we were on our own most of the time. Shawn and I swam in the local pool until dusk and played in the bike park until dark without supervision. Even while battling ear infections and bronchitis, I made every effort to keep up.

When not tagging along with my sister, I wandered through the neighborhood and surrounding area where we lived. I discovered shortcuts, trails, and even a police station. Though I passed my new school on nearly every one of my many excursions, I made no attempt to even look through the fence to catch a glimpse. The sign out front said Marvista Elementary—a name I thought was Spanish for prison.

On one particularly long walk I happened upon a large field divided by fences. Situated in a residential area, it seemed strange to see the dirt-road entrance and pastureland. I soon found out this field was actually a horse pasture, a place where I (a girl without a horse) was going to spend a lot of time in the coming months.

Not one to enjoy peace and quiet, somehow I found the calm of the horse pasture hypnotizing. I would wait for hours in the bright summer sun on the chance I would encounter a horse looking for a friend. Sometimes a horse would walk by and let me feed it grass. Even more special was when a horse and rider would come by, and I would get to talk with an actual horse owner. It might as well have been the president. I offered my services cleaning stalls in exchange for the opportunity to be near a horse. I never once asked if I could ride. I thought it was too presumptuous. Though we didn't get the newspaper, I would borrow the neighbor's and look for horses for sale. After I found good prospects I would circle them with a red ink pen. I knew I would never be able to buy one. I figured if we couldn't afford shoes, a horse was probably out of the question.

Others might have labeled my daydreaming about horses a sign I was out of touch with reality, but it was actually a great coping mechanism. I was about to encounter a lot of experiences that would not be so pleasant. When I was feeling lost, I could escape. While my daydream would change in years to come, at that point it was all about an orderly world where I had a closet full of brightly colored overalls (hanging from dark to light) and a horse in my backyard.

Looking for an Anchor

In a few months our home, school, neighborhood, friends, family structure, and everything we'd come to know had changed. Even our church, previously known for stability and comfort, was no longer available to us. It was like being without an anchor; we were adrift.

My answer for regaining my footing was, of course, cleaning.

My room no longer satisfied my thirst for order, so I took over our apartment. I used my mom's long work hours as my excuse. Rationalizing that she needed my help was better than coming to terms with the fact that I was obsessing over a toilet ring. Even I knew this was a little odd for a 10-year-old. Taking my need for order to a new level, I used whatever cleaners I could find and made a makeshift caddy out of a bucket. I gathered sponges and rags and began scrubbing at my mental pain.

Every closet and cupboard was at the mercy of my organizational whims. I would spend an hour rearranging a shelf filled with towels only to start over if the edges didn't meet perfectly or the fold of the towel wasn't precise. Rugs were straightened and straightened again and drawers were organized as if my very life depended on it. Moments of peace were fleeting as I surveyed my work. Even when everything was clean, I could not dismiss the persistent feeling that I needed to continue ordering.

SAME SONG, SECOND VERSE

When the first day of school arrived, I was nervous but kind of grateful to get out of the house. When my mom wasn't working, she was listening to sad music. After hearing Helen Reddy sing "You and Me Against the World" a zillion times, school actually started to look pretty good.

Self-sufficient at this point, I got myself dressed and fed, packed my lunch, then tidied up our apartment. After checking every appliance to ensure they were turned off and compulsively straightening the rug in the entry of our home, I placed a key around my neck and locked the door three times (you can never be too careful). Holding several notebooks and pencil boxes across my chest as if for protection, I began to walk to school.

There was a lot of excitement on the school grounds as everyone converged on the little campus of Marvista Elementary. Summer adventures were being discussed and the students were buzzing. Feeling out of place I hugged my school supplies closer.

I was the first person to walk into our classroom and sit down. Accustomed now to the back of the room, I found the seat farthest from the blackboard. I placed my supplies on top of my desk and hid behind the stack.

Kids walked into class in pairs and trios still talking, continuing their conversations from the courtyard. I stretched my legs out further so I could slump lower. Only the very top of my forehead could be seen above one of my pencil boxes.

Mr. Pike entered the room with a very stern look on his face. This guy totally knew the "don't smile until November" rule, I thought. In fact, he may have been the one who invented it. I made a mental note to ask him when I got to know him better.

Mr. Pike was a no-nonsense fella. A gentleman in his late fifties sporting a crew cut and horn-rimmed glasses, he had the most serious expression I'd ever seen. It became clear right away that Mr. Pike had made a fatal error when choosing a vocation, because apparently, he chose one he hated.

Addressing us as if we were smelly varmints with futures in

prison, Mr. Pike made little attempt to hide his disdain for the youth in front of him. As he laid out the rules of his classroom, it was clear this was going to be a long year. Don't talk, don't eat, don't chew gum, don't fidget, don't stand, don't drink from the fountain—don't, don't, don't! Did I mention he said "don't" a lot? Well, he did.

I slid further behind my pencil boxes, so far I was almost on the floor. I began feeling short of breath and started having obsessive thoughts about whether I had locked our front door.

This man seemed really irritated. Irritated teachers never liked me. Okay, let's be honest, even teachers who weren't irritated didn't like me. I was worried. Once again I was trying to figure out how this guy got here. Did someone not tell him that if he became a teacher of fifth graders, it would involve working with kids?

I would later learn that on evenings and weekends he was the manager of an old movie theater in downtown Seattle. I saw him there once and he seemed happy. He actually smiled. I didn't know until that day that the man had teeth! Well, I was much happier at the movie theater than at school too. That was the one time in a full year that I felt a sort of kinship with my teacher. The other 179 days were another story.

While sitting in the back of the class I managed to fail just about everything Mr. Pike put in front of me. Math was the worst of all subjects. The whole "don't know my times tables unless I can say all of them one through ten" was problematic. Mr. Pike was big on timed tests and I was slow as molasses. Putting my name on the board as having the lowest math scores didn't help, but Mr. Pike was convinced this would inspire me to reach my potential. I reached my potential, all right. I went on to break school records for math failure.

It took but a few weeks to be put in the lowest reading group, lowest math group, and, well, the lowest-everything group. I sat in the back of the room during lessons, then was placed in groups gathered in the back of the class to receive remedial help. I was the only student in the class to attend all of the remedial groups, a fact Mr. Pike pointed out as often as possible.

Immersed in her own problems, my mom didn't realize how bad things were at school until one day she caught a glimpse of my hands. Along with house cleaning taking a toll on my skin, I had begun washing my hands repetitively. What began as a need to "refuel" during class became an obsession. Now, both at home and at school, I couldn't seem to wash my hands enough to get them clean.

Unsure of the origin of this new compulsive behavior, she prodded until I admitted that Mr. Pike should consider quitting his day job. I didn't need to say more; my mom sprang into action. Knowing how these things usually went over, she started by writing a letter. Front-loading the letter with positive comments about his teaching style and method to throw him off guard, she gently suggested it might be better not to say negative things about me in front of the class. With an enormous amount of trepidation, I took the letter to school and gave it to Mr. Pike. When I handed it to him, he looked at it as if it were a foreign object. To help bring clarity to his confusion, I mumbled that it was from my mom. Mr. Pike nodded and promptly threw it in his desk. I saw it weeks later still in the same drawer, unopened. Apparently, he didn't appreciate letters from parents. Things got worse.

I continued to keep quiet about school because I didn't want to worry my mom. Well, truth be told, I also didn't want to have to bring another letter to school.

All my mom had to do was look at my hands and see telltale blood marks and cracks from severe dryness, and she knew. Without a word to me she made an appointment to see Mr. Pike. This time she brought cookies and opened the meeting with a conversation about the movie theater. Later she told me she had a meeting with my teacher. I was devastated but hid my immediate desire to run to the sink to start washing my hands. My mom sounded optimistic as she told me of her conversation with Mr. Pike. She said he did a lot of nodding and seemed to understand that it would be better if he didn't list my math scores on the board anymore.

When I went to school the day after "the meeting," Mr. Pike didn't say anything to me. In fact, he kind of ignored me. I was full of wishful thinking that my mom's words had softened him somehow. I washed my hands only 20 times that day.

Mr. Pike eventually resumed his guerrilla tactics, and I retreated to the sink, but for about four days there things were tolerable.

To give you an idea of how much I disliked my classroom setting, I actually began to yearn to be placed in special education. Yes, it's true! The kid who never wanted to be found out, the kid hiding behind pencil boxes in the back of the class hoping no one read her file, actually prayed someone would place her in a portable classroom out in a field.

To avoid drawing attention to my situation I actually made my way to the office one day and posed a hypothetical question to the lady behind the front desk. "If I had a friend who needed some special help because she can't read and do math very well, is there a special class that they would go to here?" I tried to make my words sound impersonal.

The receptionist put her chin to her neck, looked over her bifocals, and said, "Honey, we don't have special education classes here. Those kids go to another school." Sure I was one of "those kids," but unsure if "another school" was in Switzerland or just down the road, I decided not to press further on the issue. I resigned myself to playing with the cards I had been dealt and hoped that Mr. Pike would get a full-time job managing a theater.

The Librarian and the Dyslexic

I came to school early every day to avoid the fifth-grade boys, otherwise known as "the stinkers" who delighted in teasing me. Usually the teasing was pretty harmless stuff, but I was still scared to get to and from school.

While coming to school early was my way of avoiding unwanted teasing, it was actually a way to avoid loneliness. Always an early riser I was often up at dawn. My mom was soon off to work or involved with other tasks and my sister's school started early, so I was on my own. I prepared for school, cleaned the house, and still found myself way ahead of the clock. With no one to talk to, and uncomfortable in an empty house, I would lock and relock the door several times and head to school.

Mr. Pike did not arrive a minute before the bell, and even if he did, he was in no mood for visitors. Not knowing any of the other teachers, I wasn't sure I could just walk in, introduce myself, and hope to hide out until school began. What to do, what to do?

One particularly cold morning I stood shivering outside our classroom. Nothing stirred on our campus. I was truly alone. Or so I thought.

Right across the courtyard from our classroom was the library, and something was stirring inside. Until this time the library held no special interest for me. I could read but didn't find anything enjoyable about it. I was notorious for losing things, so I used the whole "lose a book; pay for it" rule as my excuse to avoid the place.

The library was built like a classroom but with shelves lining the walls. As I looked over, I could see a person moving around inside. To uncover the mystery I walked across the courtyard and pressed my face tightly against the window. Suddenly, the librarian popped up from behind a shelf and caught a glimpse of my face flattened on the glass. Startled, she let out a scream. Her scream made me scream and jump backward. When I jumped back, I stumbled over my books and fell over. Mrs. Carmichael opened the door and helped me off the ground. I apologized for scaring her. She told me it wasn't a problem but seemed suspicious about why I was at school so early. I made up a story about enjoying the cool air and hoped she would let me come in. Mrs. Carmichael apparently got my drift and held the door open, waving me inside.

Being inside a school building before school made me feel uncomfortable. Though I had been invited, I felt as if I were breaking a rule. Increasing my anxiety, I was in a library, a place where people went to get books. I, on the other hand, always tried to avoid books. Mrs. Carmichael ushered me over to a chair and suggested I study until school started. She clearly didn't know me. I told her I had already finished studying (failing to mention that I finished two years ago) and waited for her response.

She seemed unsure about what to do. Typically, kids weren't allowed in the buildings before school. I didn't have any schoolwork to do, so what now? Placing her hand on her chin as if it would bring her an idea, she paused. I interrupted her thoughts with a simple question: "Can I help?"

I guess Mrs. Carmichael was pretty set in her ways (or she knew I had trouble with spelling), as she seemed to find it hard to answer this question. If she had read my file, she would have eaten the words she was about to say. Ignorant of my spelling skills, she said, "Yes! I could use your help filing." I wasn't sure if I should put her in touch with Miss Derek—an individual who had learned a lesson from putting a dyslexic in charge of any sort of task involving alphabetizing. But I chose to remain silent and began a new adventure as a library assistant.

I should mention that I became a part-time employee of the school in my mind only. Mrs. Carmichael had no idea I was her assistant. I wanted to prove myself invaluable in hopes I could trade school for a full-time job in the library.

After that first day, I assumed I had a standing engagement there. While Mrs. Carmichael never turned me away, she had to keep me hidden behind bookshelves, so she wouldn't send the message to other kids that they could come in.

After some near-fatal filing problems regarding the Dewey decimal system, Mrs. Carmichael caught on to my inadequacies with symbolic language. Realizing I wasn't going to leave her side, but sure I could seriously damage anyone's ability to ever find a book again, she demoted me. It's hard to be demoted when you never really had a job, but my official duties were curtailed. To take the sting out of being fired, Mrs. Carmichael delivered a peace offering. Through several conversations that occurred while returning books to the proper shelves (well, *she* was anyway), Mrs. Carmichael learned that I spent a lot of time at the pasture and planned to buy a horse. Scouring our library for easy-reading books on the topic of horses, she hoped to pique my interest. On my next early morning visit she placed a stack of books in front of me. Hoping she was rehiring me, I was unnerved to learn she actually thought I would read them.

Strictly out of the need to be somewhere in the morning, I opened the first book. *Just look at the pictures,* I told myself. Pretend you are interested. It wasn't long before I wasn't pretending.

No doubt Mrs. Carmichael did not realize one of the books she had chosen for me would change my life. *My Winter Pony,* it was called, a story about a little girl who had a pony in her backyard. Sound familiar? The girl in the story was living my dream.

Reading about her adventures with her pony as she cared for him through a snowy winter kept me totally engaged.

Mrs. Carmichael simply may have been looking for a way to keep me busy and away from her desk, but she tapped into a proven method for coaxing even the most reluctant or resistant readers: offer text(s) about topics of interest at a reading level just below the reader's ability. I was hooked.

For the rest of the year, barring illness, I arrived early at school and sat in the library reading about horses.

FRIENDS INDEED

No longer under any sort of illusion that anyone would ever be my friend, I spent the first of many recesses at my new school on my own. I saw kids playing together and wished I could too, but I didn't expect that my social status would change anytime soon. I said very little to the kids in my class and kept my eyes averted to avoid skeptical looks they might throw in my direction.

To my complete surprise, one day three totally normal girls from my class asked if I wanted to play with them at recess. I looked over my shoulder, sure they were talking to someone else. No one was behind me so I turned my attention back to the girls. I agreed to go out to recess with them but was prepared for the inevitable brush-off.

With no peace of mind, I tagged behind the three girls toward the jungle gym. All the while I thought, *Do they not realize I'm not very smart? Well, just give them time. When they see the truth about me, they won't want to be friends with me.* As we dangled our legs through the bars, I tried to avoid saying anything stupid, so I said very little. The girls talked right over the top of my silence and didn't seem to notice I was withdrawn.

One day moved into the next and every day the same invitation came. What? Even as they saw me get assigned to remedial groups and fail one test after another, they still continued to play with me at recess. Huh?

Having managed to fend off questions about my intellect, thick glasses, and apartment status, I thought I was free. Then one rainy day, the fatal question came. In a day and age where parents seldom got divorced, and among a group of girls who didn't know anyone who was divorced, someone spoke up. "Why did you move here?" Holly asked abruptly.

Everyone looked closely at me, interested in my answer to this question. Ah, there it was—the question and answer that would send me right back to playing kick-the-can. *They made it past my glasses,* I thought, *but this is going to seal my fate.* I looked down as if the ground would provide an answer. Nothing. Wishing I could say we moved to the area due to the witness protection program, or some equally fascinating reason, I eventually had to admit that my parents were divorced and their split had prompted our move.

The group got very quiet as if contemplating what this meant. The pause in the conversation seemed like an eternity. I was preparing to go back to playing by myself again when one of the girls said, "Hey, who wants to play hopscotch?"

I thought I was now dismissed, but one of the girls, Anna, grabbed my hand and pulled me from the jungle gym. The subject was never brought up again.

From that time forward Holly, Anna, Kate, and I were friends. I was invited to their homes for after-school play dates and weekend activities. I was even invited to join their Blue Bird troop. I had no idea what a Blue Bird was, but I didn't question the invitation. Eventually, I learned that being a Blue Bird involved selling cookies and getting badges. I was not particularly good at either one of those endeavors, but I tried to remember my dues and blue vest on Tuesdays and was glad to have somewhere to go after school.

Careful not to reveal that my mom sang Helen Reddy songs repeatedly, I kept my cover, fending off requests to go to my house and play by using the excuse that nobody was home. Though I knew nothing was perfect, I was convinced that my friends were better off than I and wouldn't understand my situation if they saw it up close.

DATING AND OTHER BAD IDEAS

I knew the minute my dad left that we were in trouble. Struggling financially was just the tip of the iceberg; my mom was kind of lost. I think if she would have taken time to heal, we all would have been better off. Instead, she hastily looked for a solution to her loneliness. No doubt God was crying out to her and saying, "Take care of yourself!"

We would later learn she thought she was being told, "Get

married in a big fat hurry to the first person you meet!" It's just a guess, but I am pretty sure that message didn't come from God.

A few months into the school year my mom was seeing a fellow who never smiled. She shined him up to be perfect. My mom could do that, you know—make something iffy look swell. This resourceful trait might work well when reviewing your boss, but it isn't recommended when sizing up a boyfriend. I could not understand decimal numbers to save my life, but even I knew Bill was not a catch.

It wasn't long before we were informed my mom and Bill were going to get married. This meant we would be moving at the end of the school year. My sister and I tried to look for alternatives. My sister was happy in her school. I had three friends, not counting Mrs. Carmichael. Neither of us wanted to go, but my mom would hear none of it. With her mind set, we began packing boxes.

This was going to be an "I told you so" moment, or series of moments. Two years' worth of moments to be exact. One of those segments of life where my mom would look back and say, "What was I thinking?"

Mom could not have been thinking straight. Bill was in need of a toupee and contact lenses. Soon she would make sure he had both, but these changes improved only the exterior. All he had to do was open his mouth to reveal the truth. Off-color jokes and a crude sense of humor seemed out of place coming from a man with an advanced degree in a respected profession. Time would reveal, though, that this was a man struggling with mental illness and a violent temper. With no faith in God as his guide, he was extremely unpredictable and a constant source of anxiety for me. Since he roamed the house without a shirt and erupted over the littlest thing, we quickly learned never to invite anyone to our home.

Bill had two children, a seven-year-old boy who lived with his mother and a fourteen-year-old daughter who lived with him. While the boy seemed well-adjusted, the daughter seemed much younger than her years. She always spoke in a low whisper, and with her slumped shoulders and timid smile, she seemed troubled. Eventually, we would learn the truth about Lisa, but for now her father insisted that a bitter divorce and rejection by her mother had left her damaged.

Ever "the fixer," Mom thought she could help Lisa overcome her challenges by redecorating her room. If only it were that simple. But gingham curtains don't heal the kind of wounds Lisa carried.

As the end of the school year approached, my hands were raw and my nerves were frayed. I kept hoping there would be a reprieve, some chance my mom would come to her senses. As each day passed, though, it seemed to only steel her resolve to move forward with her plans.

On the last day of school I said good-bye to Mrs. Carmichael and told my friends I hoped to see them again. I was only moving about 20 miles away, I reasoned. Surely we could still keep in touch. I made no attempt to avoid the bullies on my way home from school, so heavy was my heart. As one of them yelled, "Where are you going, four-eyes?" I didn't even look up.

In my backpack was a report card that said, "Shari is making progress. Best wishes in your new school." Apparently Mr. Pike believed in social promotion (moving a kid forward in school based on age and not academic progress) or he was just grateful to see me go. I was so absorbed in feelings of loss that my usual preoccupation with what was going to happen the next school year didn't even cross my mind. When my mom read my report card, she was relieved to see I had passed. I knew I was not doing well enough in school to move to the next grade, but for the first time in many years, I truly didn't care.

Within days after school got out, we filled a U-Haul and were on our way to a new apartment. In an effort to be closer to Bill, Mom moved us to the city where he lived. By August, against the wishes of every family member familiar with the situation, my mom got remarried. We stayed with my grandparents while my mom and Bill went on their honeymoon. Upon their return we moved into Bill's house. My mom put up lots of curtains and rearranged furniture in every room hoping to breathe life into the space, but no matter what she did, the same uncomfortable feeling hung in the air.

Not long after my mom and Bill got married, Bill lost his job. The irony is intense here. My mom got married for love and validation, but also because she might have been scared about making it on her own. Now, aside from some unemployment, she was the sole breadwinner for a family of six. With my stepdad out of work, my mom was forced to take second and third jobs to keep us afloat. Because my mom was not around much to protect us, I learned to stay away.

The only thing Bill ever did for me was to get me a puppy—

a mutt that peered from the bottom of a cardboard box with the word "free" on the flap. This tiny dog with a severe under bite was my very good friend. Together we roamed our new neighborhood looking for reasons not to go home.

8

On the Other Side of the Tracks

A hasty remarriage landed me in a new school assigned to a class-room with an emotionally absent teacher. Accustomed to being ostracized for a low IQ, I now found new reasons to be on the out-side. Labeled "from the other side of the tracks," I came to believe that Nike tennis shoes and a pair of contact lenses would save my life. With my home life in disarray, I hid in my room hoping some-thing would change.

School was about to begin, but I had only just moved into the district. Keep this in mind as I tell you the sordid tale of my sixth-grade year.

When we arrived at Clyde Hill Elementary to register for school, the campus looked like any other. With architecture that was square and tidy, nothing seemed out of the ordinary. The office smelled sort of musty with an aroma of paste.

I shifted my feet around as my stepdad filled out my paperwork. I wished my mom was there with me, but she was working that day. If she had been there, she would have made small talk and complimented the secretary on her blouse or lapel pin. She would have brought cookies and presents hoping to win over a few hearts. My mom had become a master at the "art of negotiation." She knew I was a tough fit in any classroom, so she would begin begging, pleading, and cajoling early so I wouldn't end up getting held back, kicked out, or placed with the weird teacher who told kids they were stupid. Not so long before, she had been bent on saving me from untold disaster at school; now, she was just glad I was passing. With too many brush fires in our personal lives and too many bills to pay, I slowly lost my advocate. Because my mom wasn't there to "pitch" for me, I was going to go where there was space, not to a class that was the best place for me. I'm glad I didn't see what was coming.

You see, we had no clout and no capital at this school. I was just another kid with a mom who was trying her best. We were not connected. Kids who are not "connected"—those with parents who either can't or don't know how to advocate for them—end up in what I have politely labeled "the crack." (That's my way of describing a classroom where the teacher would rather be managing a movie theater.) This crack is the crack referred to in the comment, "That kid is falling through the cracks." This familiar phrase refers to multiple cracks of different origins. I was actually falling into a bona fide gully, a gaping hole in the Bell

Public School system called a fifth/sixth split featuring an emotionally bankrupt teacher named Mr. Boise.

While enrolling me, Bill grumbled over questions about vac-
cinations and pediatricians. He knew nothing about my vaccina-
tion history, so I don't know how he managed to turn in my
paperwork. As the woman behind the desk looked over my
forms, I bit my lip nervously and stared at the floor, hoping and
praying Bill wouldn't open his mouth. While he had been my
stepdad for less than 30 days, his ability to be offensive was
already clear to me. I was hoping we could escape quickly before
he cracked a joke.

As we were leaving, I looked over the secretary's shoulder
and saw a large room stuffed with file cabinets. At one time I
would have wanted to run into that room, steal my file, and
burn it. Now I was numb to its contents. It didn't seem like it
mattered anymore.

When my mom got home, I told her I was in a split class
and that my teacher's name was Raymond Boise. "That's great,"
Mom said with halfhearted enthusiasm. I could tell she wasn't
listening. My stepdad was roaming around the kitchen without a
shirt, and my sister was expecting a guest. Frantically my mom
hurried to soothe Bill's psyche hoping to coax him into some
clothes.

"Isn't there a city named Boise?" I continued as I opened the
refrigerator. No response came from my mom. I turned around
to see that everyone was gone, probably off to find a shirt. I realized I had been talking to myself and decided to go talk to my
dog. Scotty, always a willing listener, appeared to be interested as

I told him of a split class, a concept for which I had no frame of reference, and a teacher with a name like a city.

On the first day of school I had a small anxiety attack about the new school, but after making my bed several times I was able to gather myself. I got dressed and made my lunch, then sat on the edge of my bed, overly prepared. I realized I had an hour before I was supposed to leave for the bus stop. After washing my hands repeatedly and rearranging my closet, it was finally time to go.

I walked with great trepidation from our home on South Point Lane to the bus stop, only a few blocks away. To ease my spirit I said a prayer and then made every attempt to avoid all cracks in the sidewalk along the way.

The significance of my street name had not become totally clear to me, but it soon would. "South Point Lane" was a small side street lined with modest homes, just off a long road lined with multimillion-dollar estates called South Point. Most of the kids from South Point did not ride the bus; their drivers took them to school. Even at the bus stop there was a clear delineation of status and class.

Prior to this I had paid no attention to what people wore or the symbols on their clothes or shoes. Maybe it wasn't as big an issue in the places I had lived, or maybe it was because I was so busy trying to hide or keep up that I didn't have time to worry about the brand name on my jeans. I was blissfully ignorant about socioeconomic status and everything that it meant, and I didn't fully realize how the world viewed me. But the labels used to categorize me were growing: *child of divorce, latchkey kid, learning disabled, at risk,* and now add *lower-socioeconomic status, unemployed, second marriage,* and *stepchild.* It was a lot simpler when I was just the kid they called *special.*

Soon I would have to spend time making my shoes dirty so I could disguise the K-Mart label and fear ridicule because I wore generic pants. There would be days when kids I wished to play with, who lived but a few blocks away from my home, would tell me that their parents would not let them because I lived on "the lane." The gap between me and other kids would become wide, but it was more than intellectual now.

Always the early bird, I was alone at the bus stop for several minutes before anyone else arrived. By the time the bus pulled up, at least 20 kids had gathered. All of them seemed to know each other. I sat alone on the bus. After each stop the bus filled up more, but curiously, the seat next to me remained empty. Finally, with no room left on the bus, one rider had no choice and sat next to me, leaning away to be sure I knew it was out of necessity she took the seat. At first I thought this was just run-of-the-mill ostracism. It happened to me all the time, so I knew what it looked like. I didn't realize it wasn't just because I was wearing humongous blue glasses. (Here's a tip: Don't let your mother pick out your eyewear.) It was about the tag on my tennis shoes.

"Other" Wing People

After a crowded bus ride I entered a breezeway following a crowd of kids toward a cluster of buildings. With no sense of direction, I often didn't know where I was going and would just blend into the crowd and move. The problem is, I didn't always end up where I wanted to be. Getting lost was a great way to miss class during math, but on this day I was truly looking forward to seeing my classroom. I just happened to follow the right group, and the kids led me straight to a wing of the school located next to a playfield. Once inside I learned this was the sixth-grade wing.

As I walked down the hall, there was a special feeling in the air—lots of excitement. Kids actually looked really happy to be there. I overhead a few students talking about something called the "sixth-grade team." Eventually I learned that this "team" was actually made up of all the sixth-grade classes. The team of sixth graders went on field trips and had parties and special events together.

Unsure of where my classroom was, I asked someone who looked like a teacher for directions to Mr. Boise's room. The teacher was polite but seemed distant. I was informed that Mr. Boise was in "another wing" on the other side of the school. He said "another wing" like he had just tasted something bad. I might have been dreaming, but it seemed as if he wanted to spit.

Not only had the teacher's demeanor when speaking about "another wing" gotten me worried, I was altogether confused why I—a sixth grader—would not be in the sixth-grade wing with all the other sixth graders. I walked out of the building with a concerned expression hoping this would have a good ending.

It turned out my class really was in "another wing" on the other side of the school. Our wing looked just like the sixth-grade building but had a decidedly different feel. It was comprised of two empty double classrooms used for storage, a set of bathrooms, a second and third grade double classroom, and a fifth-grade class. Right in the middle of the building was my room: Mr. Boise's fifth/sixth split. This "open concept" modular classroom had no formal door, just an open space in a wall partition. I peeked around the "wall" into a huge classroom made up of a wall of windows, a work area in the back, and desks up front. A red-haired, bearded man was standing at the back of the room drinking a hot cup of something while watching kids enter the room. With no seating chart, kids were able to choose their seats. As usual I made my way to the back.

When I was really little I would have made up a good story about why I was separated. I would have said, "I am so special that I am going to special education; I am so elevated in my skills I need to go to a special classroom," and so on. Unfortunately, I was smart enough now to know the truth. As I sat down in the "not-sixth-grade wing," I felt crushed with shame.

I knew how things worked. Someone had read my file and thought I was not sixth-grade material. My scores from the previous year were awful. The whole "Shari is making progress" comment from Mr. Pike upon my exit from Marvista wouldn't have fooled the powers-that-be. No doubt the decision makers placed me in a split class made up primarily of fifth graders (of 25 kids, only four were sixth graders) so I wouldn't have to be held back. I felt a rush of sweat on the back of my neck, and tears burned in my eyes. I wanted to run home, but had no idea where or in which direction home was.

It turns out that Mr. Boise had previously sued the school after being fired for misconduct. To avoid a lawsuit the school district rehired him. What a glowing endorsement. Where do you sign up for his class?

Our room was built with an open concept in mind. Collapse the walls and eliminate doors. Freedom of thought and freedom of movement—just perfect for someone with ADHD.

In the spirit of free thought, Mr. Boise told students to go at their own paces in all subject areas. Super! I can do that. He said, "Go at your own pace," but I thought he was talking about exercise. I spent most of the next year out in our hallway going at my own pace. When not in the hallway I was hiding in the bathroom waiting for the bell to ring. The weirdest thing of all is that no one came looking for me. Ever!

Now it all makes sense: If you have an open-concept classroom, you don't actually have to teach. No wonder Mr. Boise preferred this format. Most of his time was consumed with burning incense or something like it, drinking tea, and observing us going at our own paces. He would sit in the back of the room staring out over his mug. On the rare occasions we were required (I use that term loosely) to do something academic, I made little progress.

The rest of the year we were treated to all kinds of antics but very little real teaching. We spent—and I am not exaggerating—six months learning where babies come from. What if you don't want to know? Mr. Boise was so zealous in his quest to make sure we were all completely grossed out and/or embarrassed that to top off our unit on the birds and the bees, he brought in a video of a woman giving birth—information I would have enjoyed not knowing until I actually gave birth. By the way, we shared the birthing-video-experience with the fifth-grade class next to us. Lucky them. I am sure if they had wanted to join us, Mr. Boise would have been more than happy to share the video with the second and third grade classes across the hall. Maybe they heard it anyway; after all, we didn't have doors.

Somehow I survived that year. The librarian was a really nice fellow who showed me how to use these little comic-strip-type movies. With no desire to go out to recess, I would hide out in the library. I do not recall taking one book off the shelf. I just remember the movies I watched at recess. My other angel was a paraprofessional who served as a teacher's aide in our classroom. On the few occasions we did anything academic, I spent class time permanently planted at her makeshift desk. I knew I was struggling and so did she, but she never lost patience with me as she answered the same questions over and over again.

Socially, I was an outcast. I had developed a film of small blemishes on my skin that seemed to worsen if I drank milk. My nose was still running, and my glasses, well, did I mention they were blue? I had begged every doctor I had seen since the age of three to please give me contact lenses. In fifth grade a specialist said the nature of my eye problems made it impossible for me to ever wear contacts. We went to another specialist in sixth grade. He said the same thing. I was devastated. I was crying too hard to pick out a pair of frames. Fatal mistake! Thus, the blue glasses. My mom meant well.

It is funny how you pin all of your hopes and dreams on one

thing. I thought contacts would change my life completely. I guess I thought that if I got rid of my glasses, people wouldn't notice my high-water pants and frizzy hair. What?

Did I mention I was the only girl to play the drums in the band my sixth-grade year? I signed up as soon as I heard you got to miss class a couple of times a week. Why the snare drum? Maybe I thought that banging on something would be perfect for a hyperactive kid. My mom agreed and rented me a drum; then she quickly returned to the store and got a rubber top to dampen the sound while I practiced at home. Lack of private lessons put me at a disadvantage with kids who had been playing for several years. (Well, that's what I told myself.) In truth, I lacked hand-eye coordination. Oh, and the whole can't-read-music thing presented a problem. I was relegated to the bass drum at the spring concert. One, two, three, bang. One, two, three, bang.

I will say that taking a snare drum to school a couple of times a week really got me noticed. Now I was the girl from "the lane" who was weird and played the drums: a lethal combination if you ever wanted to fit in. On band days I would limp to the bus stop carrying my heavy drum case. The only blessing was that I would sit my drum next to me, so that I wouldn't have to endure people avoiding me on the bus.

Oh, one other thing: My mom had tried to correct my chlorine-soaked hair by bleaching it. Um, she made me a platinum blonde. With the damage to my hair and roots coming in dark, she was unsure about what to do next. So she kept bleaching it. As if the kids at school didn't have enough to work with. I had frizzy, out-of-control hair the color of Jean Harlow's. My color would have looked perfect on a 50-year-old woman. One last thing: Even though I was blonde, I had thick, dark eyebrows. If I had a dime for every time someone asked me, "Do you bleach your hair?" I would be a rich woman. I was so embarrassed about my hair that I lied and said I didn't bleach my hair. I know, lying is sin, but for some reason I got the impression that admitting I bleached my hair was worse than lying about it. Lying only served to invigorate those taunting me.

So I watched movies at recess and sat alone on the bus. I was in the forgotten "other wing" with third graders. Thankfully, I knew where babies came from.

I may have been a social pariah with learning disabilities, but I was unsure what bad luck had led these other poor souls (the kids in my class) into this black hole (our classroom). I secretly believed that either they were slow and someone read their file, or their parents really blew it at registration.

Sometimes I would look longingly at the sixth-grade wing and wish I could be a part of it. It was kind of like shopping with no money, seeing something really neat that I couldn't touch. Knowing that even if I was in the sixth-grade wing, I probably wouldn't be accepted didn't deter me from longing for it. Strangely, the handful of sixth graders in our split class never interacted with the other kids from the sixth-grade wing. At first I thought it was just a coincidence that no one in our class knew those kids. Over time, though, it became clear that they avoided us. We were the "other wing" people.

With only the kids in our classroom to interact with, I felt sure I was going to be alone. Then one day, for some unknown reason, a totally nice, popular, fifth-grade girl who happened to be in my class (what did her parents do wrong at registration?) talked to me. I was totally caught off guard. *Why would she talk to me? Doesn't she know that I have blue glasses and platinum hair?*

Cali was the kind of girl destined for the sixth-grade wing, if you get my drift. This whole fifth/sixth split was just a momentary stopover on her way to greatness. I was totally mystified that she would consider playing with me. Well, let me clarify: She didn't play with me at recess, but during class she would. I know, kind of a double standard, right?

When the rainy season came, Cali didn't go out to play with her friends anymore and was willing to stay inside with me. Having options beyond hiding in the library was great. Cali and I would play in the storage room next to our classroom creating elaborate plays and skits. One of our creations was a joke and magic show. With the goal of presenting the show to the second and third grade classrooms across the hall (whether they wanted to watch it or not), we set to work in earnest.

My mom lent us clown costumes she had used during lean times to make extra money from children's parties. The outfits were too big for us, but we used rubber bands and paper clips to make alterations. Using an open cubical as a backdrop and some crates as a stage, we perfected our script and planned for our show date.

Bags of balloons in hand, we presented the "Shari and Cali Joke Show" to thunderous applause. Well, it may have been the sound of one hand clapping, but that is just because little kids aren't that coordinated. We were sure it was a hit. I was ready to quit school and take our show on the road.

Desperate to share the success of the day, I couldn't wait to get home. As I approached our driveway, I saw my stepdad's truck. I was crushed. I knew that if my stepdad's truck was there and my mom's station wagon wasn't, that I should not go in the house. This was an unspoken rule I had developed. Even if I had to go to the bathroom, even if I was hungry or cold, I wouldn't go into the house.

Leaving my book bag on the doorstep, I unlocked my dog's kennel and hugged him. As we walked over to the construction site next door, I filled Scotty in on everything that had happened. When Mom finally pulled into the driveway, it was dark. I burst through the door to tell her my good news and became keenly aware of problems in the air. Bill was once again without a shirt and was yelling because someone chipped a dish. The tirade lasted well into the night. My mom was trying to deflect his anger, searching for a way to calm the situation. Knowing this was not a good time to talk about the joke show, I slipped past the argument and ducked into my room. Closing the door behind me, I soothed my mind by organizing my doll collection. I turned up the small black-and-white television set in my room to drown out the sound of the argument, then fell into a troubled sleep. I awoke early the next morning to a test pattern.

Still feeling good about the day before, I knew I'd get the opportunity to tell my mom about the joke show's success. I peeked out of my room to see if my stepdad was at the kitchen table. He must have been sleeping late, no doubt tired from ranting and raving. Hoping to catch my mom before she went to work, I snuck around the house on tiptoe. On my way through the kitchen I saw the chipped dish that had sparked the chaos the night before and shook my head. *What a waste,* I thought. With no sight of Mom in the house, I ran to the porch hoping to see her car. It was gone. Discouraged, I promised myself I would talk to my mom that night.

I returned to school feeling tired and uneasy. I missed my mom and wished things could be different at home. I looked forward to seeing Cali. I was deeply upset when I got to school and learned she was absent. I went to the bathroom and cried. Who knows how long I stayed there.

While Mr. Boise was not an evil man, he was not someone I respected. The whole "sex education thing" was one of many clues that this man had issues. While hiding behind a '60s exterior and a sort of "free your mind" mantra, he was actually a true passive-aggressive. When I first entered his class, I sat in the back but made numerous attempts to get his attention. I approached his desk, tried to start conversations—anything to get attention. I no longer fell off my chair or cracked jokes, but sat still and hoped for his praise. Longing for a mentor who could give me what I was missing at home, I looked in the wrong place; my teacher was indifferent and made me feel invisible. The social experiment going on in our classroom was confirmed when Mr. Boise chose to end my friendship with Cali. I have searched my heart repeatedly, wondering why a teacher would do what my teacher did, and to this day I have no answer.

One day during reading I was called up to Mr. Boise's desk. I was caught off guard when he stated it was unhealthy for me to have just one friend. He told me I needed to branch out and find new people to play with. Short, sweet, and to-the-point. Stunned, I opened my mouth to say, "But I can't make other friends," but he waved me quiet with his hand and sent me back to my desk. Cali was then called up to his desk. A brief conversation ensued. I thought this was some kind of cruel joke and I looked at my friend to see her reaction. She looked at me, then looked away. Though I tried to speak to her at recess, she politely refused to talk. Our friendship was over.

I have no idea what Mr. Boise said to her, but my imagination ran wild. By the afternoon recess I was so out of sorts that I wandered the playground crying.

I walked to the end of our lower playfield and stood on the boundary line between our school and the junior high. Just beyond the trees I could see kids running the track, and I thought for sure I saw my sister. Though I knew crossing the boundary was a huge infraction, I ran toward the track of the junior high not caring about consequences. Stopping after a few yards, I reached the track. I searched the faces of the runners, looking for Shawn. A brown-haired girl passed, but it wasn't her. Realizing that my sister was not on the field, I slumped down on my heels. I did not want to go back to school, and I did not want to go back to my class. I wondered how far I would get if I started running.

Just then a playground monitor from my school tapped me on the shoulder. She didn't look too pleased. She said, "You are not supposed to be here. Come with me." I followed her right to a chair outside the principal's office. I was hoping to be expelled.

Instead of being expelled I was given a worse fate. After a stern talking to, I was sent back to Mr. Boise.

With a few months remaining in the school year I returned to watching comic strips at recess and hiding in the bathroom. Aside from when my dad left, there had never been a lower point in my life.

I stopped taking the bus. I needed to get out of the house early to avoid the fighting, so I walked a considerable distance to school. Our library was open, and I spent time there or walked around the playground. I was so lonely it felt physically painful.

I was never so glad to see a school year come to an end. I was pretty sure I would be passing to seventh grade since the only standard was going at your own pace.

HOLDING ON

Looking back on this time I wonder what kept me going. I had no friends, there was increasing turbulence at home, and I had no real academic success, yet I believed if I just prayed more, God would save me. It never occurred to me that life wasn't worth living or that I should attempt to leave the world; that's due to my early church experiences. I had little Bible knowledge, but I did know that God had overcome the world and there was nothing I faced that He couldn't help me through. If it had not been for my faith I might have just been another kid that didn't want to go on. Instead, even in my sadness, I kept cleaning and praying, cleaning and praying, and hoping for miracles.

Ironically, just down a flight of stairs in our home sat my stepsister contemplating the first of several suicide attempts. Lisa was lovely, but fractured. She had made great strides to move forward in her life and with support from my sister and mom, she lost weight and improved her manner of dress. But this was only window dressing. Years of verbal abuse and rejection from her mom and an extremely unhealthy relationship with her dad darkened her heart. She could tag along with my sister to gain access to a new crowd, but it didn't change the fact that she hated herself.

My mom saved her twice and managed to get her into counseling, but there had been so much damage before we ever arrived that every intervention seemed trivial.

With my stepsister's condition worsening, it seemed strange that my mom would send Lisa and me to stay with my step-grandparents for the summer. I was told I could get a job picking strawberries and could make extra money for school clothes. Enticed by the idea of buying a pair of Nike tennis shoes, I said yes. This is a kid who had never been to a sleepover. I had never been to camp. I had never been away from home. Kids will do crazy things to not have their shoes draw attention. The fact that my stepgrandparents had a pony sweetened the deal.

Little did I know that my mom was attempting to remove Lisa from the psychological warfare of her parents and save me from my stepdad's increasingly volatile temper.

While being free of my stepdad sounded good, I ended up living in an RV with what I didn't understand at the time was a stepsister on the brink of disaster. All I knew was that she was sad and angry most of the time. I learned to stay out of her way and escape to the pasture.

At the end of that summer, I returned home to no fanfare. It was almost as though no one had noticed I was gone. My mom had gained 50 pounds and aged several years. Things were getting worse.

After a hot, sweaty summer in the berry fields, I earned enough money to buy my tennis shoes. With my Nikes and a pair of contact lenses (thanks to a new specialist), I was going to enter seventh grade with a whole new outlook. Just when things were looking up, my mom tried to tone down my platinum hair and accidentally turned it gray. I went to my first day of school looking like I should apply for Medicare.

9

I Can't See College from Here

While I arrived at school early and stayed late to avoid going home, I did nothing productive with my time. My philosophy of life had become solidified: Don't try and then you really haven't failed. Though I had completely given up on myself, some teachers would show me that I could learn a different way.

Squinting with pain due to new hard contact lenses and looking as if I should receive a senior discount, I entered seventh grade with guarded optimism. At this point, getting out of our house the maximum number of hours allowed each day was my primary motivation for going to school. While not my first choice, school was safer than a street corner. Though nothing about me suggested I was motivated or even interested in school, I was just covering up. I would have done anything to do well; I just didn't think it was possible. I truly didn't know how to succeed.

Preparing to reprise my role as the incredible shrinking kid, I planned to sit in the back and perfect the art of counting ceiling tiles. Keep quiet, stay low, and maybe—just maybe—I could get by without being noticed. The truth is, I was desperate, hungry, and longing for positive attention.

Before school started, my mom took my sister and me aside and whispered a desperate admonition. She firmly demanded that we not repeat her mistakes and advised us that education and college provided a chance for a better life. My sister was already preparing to go to college, her sights set on the University of Washington. I stayed quiet during this discussion knowing I would be lucky to get out of seventh grade. Seeing the pain in my mom's eyes, I said a silent prayer for some kind of transformation.

Believing academic goals were out of reach, I would have settled for popularity. Now I thank God every day that no one liked me then. I could have made some serious mistakes by confusing *being liked* with *being successful.* God took away peer pressure when He took away peers. Oh, the things we don't understand until after the fact. I was wishing for friends, while God was protecting me from something worse than loneliness. With no distractions, no activities, and no social opportunities there was plenty of time to be found, redirected, and nurtured. At a time when statistics suggest that kids can't change, I was about to discover I could be more than a failure.

No doubt I left educators wondering about me—a goofy kid

who appeared to not be paying attention. I didn't intend to
ignore them, but whatever tricks I had used to "appear focused"
no longer worked. I was in some kind of heightened state of distraction. My books were heavy; I couldn't remember my locker
combination; I got lost finding my classrooms; I was disorganized and didn't have my stuff; by the time I found my stuff, the
class was over and the whole cycle would start again. With a bigger school and a different system, I just couldn't seem to get my
act together. Well, it isn't like I *ever* had my act together, but let's
just say I was even more discombobulated.

Another obstacle to any type of classroom success was the
fact that I had been coasting for the better part of three years.
Since fourth grade I had not developed any deep-rooted organizational, let alone academic, skills. What I had perfected was
how to procrastinate and/or make excuses for not doing my
work, turning in late work, or turning in work that was not up
to standard. Oh, and we all know I was good at going at my
own pace—another way of saying "doing nothing."

Teachers in Magic Capes

Unaware of my surroundings, I truly had entered the land of
giants. Thinking it was just another year, I would soon encounter
dedicated teachers who were about to change my life: a PE
teacher who managed to make this uncoordinated klutz feel good
about herself, never wincing when I fell over my own feet; a chorus teacher who discovered I couldn't read music but made it
seem like an asset that I learned songs by ear; a saintly biology

teacher who made atoms interesting; a French teacher who, upon hearing me butcher even the simplest words, remained convinced that I could become bilingual. (I was appreciative of her belief in me, but convinced I couldn't master the language. I kept coming to class sure that learning how to say, "Where's the bathroom?" in French might come in handy someday.) Last, but certainly not least, came two individuals who must be mentioned by name: Mr. Parcin—my language arts and social studies teacher—and Mrs. Ells—my math teacher. Both were educators fashioned in the style of Miss Derek, a kind of take-no-prisoners, Ninja tag team missing only their magic capes. They had my number right from the start. Managing to do the unthinkable, they made me feel as if school was worth fighting for.

Mrs. Ells could look over her glasses while writing on the overhead projector, throw you a look that could kill, and never break stride with her explanation of addition of like-denominator fractions. As the recipient of several of those looks, I quickly respected her. Looking like you are paying attention in class, however, is very different from actually paying attention. Just when I thought I had her fooled, she changed the seating chart. I was all smug in my seat behind the kid who must have been held back twice, thinking my thoughts could drift out the window. Mrs. Ells would have none of it. Suddenly there I was with a new seat in the front of the room. My cover was blown. The kid who had been held back twice was now sitting next to me. We gave each other knowing glances and succumbed to math boot camp.

Mrs. Ells was no shrinking violet. Like a drill sergeant in

elastic-waistband pants, she was going to make sure that every kid left her class knowing the definition of a polynomial. I had all kinds of excuses, and they fell on deaf ears. All she had to do was look over her glasses and say, "Miss Rusch, who do you think you are talking to?" Interrupted in mid-excuse about my stolen homework, I would plop into my seat and attempt to keep my eyes on my desk.

Often Mrs. Ells would call my name in a loud voice, startling me into looking up. Tapping on the overhead, she'd ask, "Are you with us, Miss Rusch?"

I snapped to attention and said, "Yes!" simply out of fear. She proceeded to ask me the answer to the question on the overhead. Having just joined the lesson and without notes to help, I was at a loss for words. I doled out a half-baked response. With pursed lips and a "we'll discuss this later" look, she moved on to the next victim—I mean, student. Thinking my discomfort with being unprepared would lead me to change my behavior, Mrs. Ells soon came to the realization that I didn't understand I was part of the problem. Apparently I thought coming unprepared to class, making up excuses, not doing my homework, and not bringing the things I needed to function in class were just part of the whole "I have learning disabilities" thing. My teacher wasn't buying it.

Fed up with me, she finally called me to her desk and asked, "Where are your supplies?"

"Supplies?" I said, as if I had never heard the word before.

"Yes, supplies," Mrs. Ells said with a bit of frustration.

"I don't have any," I said, hoping that answer would prevent me from having to do anything for the rest of the year.

"Get me your book bag," Mrs. Ells said in a somber voice.

"Okay," I said nervously.

After looking in my bag she realized that, in fact, I didn't have any supplies. I had left them in my locker for good measure.

Feeling a strange sort of relief, I gathered my book bag and headed to my desk. "Miss Rusch," Mrs. Ells said in a more frustrated tone, "you will come to my class with the proper supplies from this time forward. Paper, pencil, eraser, notebook. These are things you are required to have when you get here tomorrow."

I sensed she meant what she said. A bead of sweat was on her upper lip. She stared at me intently. "Do you get what I am saying?"

I started to say something about having a hard time remembering what I needed and getting from my locker to class with the right stuff. She stopped me mid-sentence and said, "If you can't get from your locker to class with your supplies and on time, then don't go to your locker."

"What?" I said, kind of confused.

"Don't go to your locker. Carry everything you need with you for all of your classes." She said this last sentence really abruptly as if to cut off my next excuse. I could tell the conversation was over. I returned to my seat.

Thinking I was finished with Mrs. Ells, I was surprised to see her walk over to my desk and place a brand-new number two pencil and a pad of paper in front of me. She looked me in the eye and said, "You can do this. Don't make excuses." She put her hand on my shoulder, gave it a firm squeeze, and walked away. That was the moment she became my friend.

The next day I came to class with a book bag as big as me, but on time and ready with my supplies, by golly. Her admonition may have caused me a backache, but it was the right thing to do. Returning to my locker between each class was a luxury I couldn't afford. I couldn't remember my locker combination most of the time and got lost often. I decided to take my teacher's advice, and it worked. An approving look from Mrs. Ells fueled me to keep my book bag flung over my shoulder and to avoid my locker bay.

Though really good at rearranging stuff on my desk ad nauseam to calm my nerves and fully distract me from what my teacher was saying, I had never applied any of my organizational skills in a useful way to school. I cannot explain why someone who can color code a sock drawer in 30 seconds flat would have a notebook that looked like a bomb went off. A convenient excuse for failure because it was better than being considered slow, being disorganized had become another one of my covers. With paper-hole reinforcers in hand, Mrs. Ells was about to change all that.

One day my book bag accidentally tipped over, and a massive pile of papers, books, pencils, and school gear tumbled onto the floor. Hearing the landslide Mrs. Ells took one look at the mess and called me over. She said, "This simply will not do." I looked around the room as if to feign ignorance and pretended not to understand her meaning.

Pointing her finger to the floor, she said again, "This simply will not do!" with more emphasis. I looked at the mess on the floor and realized the jig was up. She went on, "Miss Rusch, you need to get things in order!" I knew just enough about Mrs. Ells by now to realize she wasn't going to let me off with an excuse about being organizationally challenged due to a full moon. She meant business. Now what?

One piece of paper at a time, one section of my notebook at a time, Mrs. Ells helped me purge what I didn't need and organize what I did need. A few new folders added, a few more paper-hole reinforcers applied, and suddenly I had a notebook worthy of notice. Placing everything in my book bag according to the order of my classes made my supplies and school materials easy to find. Used to confusion and chaos lurking everywhere, I felt a strange sense of calm. As with lines on the floor or order in my dresser drawers, organization helped my mind feel swept, and I started to feel at ease.

After organizing my book bag and notebook, Mrs. Ells made sure I had a calendar of homework assignments, quizzes, and tests. Winging it had always been the best way to avoid accountability. I couldn't remember the quiz was coming, so I didn't have to study for it. My first reaction to the calendar was dismay—my excuse was now gone—but in time it actually gave me a sense of control, and I realized that I did not need to fail by default.

Once organized, I discovered a variety of basic skills to address before I could ever hope to succeed. Simple things like raising my hand had long been forgotten.

I used to raise my hand in class just for the fun of it, waving so wildly that no one could miss me. I also employed sound effects to ensure maximum exposure. Somewhere along the way the crazy kid who nearly fell off her chair to get attention had been lost in the back of the room. So sure that I had nothing of value to offer, I let my hand become heavily weighted. Just the thought of raising it made my shoulder ache.

Mrs. Ells could see my resistance. It takes courage to face silence and a classroom of eyes as you stutter through what could potentially be a wrong answer or a dumb question. Still she insisted that I try to raise my hand and contribute in class. She protected me by politely moving on to someone else if my blank look indicated that the mere act of putting my hand down after being called on had caused me to forget what I was about to say. Even with faulty results, raising my hand meant that I was going to get a participation grade—a huge step for a kid used to hiding.

On to note-taking, a phrase I thought meant writing everything down as fast as you could, then giving up when you got tired. My hand could never keep up with someone's voice. I wrote slowly and had trouble spelling. If I used some kind of shorthand, I found it difficult to decode what I had written. Even when there was a visual aid to assist me, my eyes didn't track well, making it nearly impossible to transfer information from the blackboard or overhead to my paper. My response to this conundrum? Don't take notes. Perfect logic, right?

Mrs. Ells had to teach me how to take notes all over again, encouraging me to write only what was most important and teaching me how to determine what that was. She asked me to work a little harder on my penmanship skills so my notes were readable. *Readable* doesn't mean *spelled correctly*, by the way. Just as Miss Derek did, Mrs. Ells had to prioritize. My spelling was so bad, she just tried to get me to write legibly. I broke some serious lead trying to please her but got praise by the bucketload when my paper didn't look like an excuse for bad art. She even had to teach me how to lay out my notes so the paper was organized. I would write information all over the place, then wonder why I couldn't move step-by-step through a problem. When the answer is at the top of the page and the question is at the bottom, it is hard to retrace your steps—another great excuse for failure foiled by Mrs. E.

If anyone could be effective in teaching me, it would be Mrs. Ells. She was repetitive and methodical in the way she presented her material. Say it, write it (on the overhead so you have a visual), and say it again (exactly the same way), and then say it again while pointing to what she had written. It may not have been flashy, but I seldom got lost. Step-by-step she walked us through problems, and the way she presented the material made it seem less abstract.

Mrs. Ells made me think of learning, especially a concept as difficult as math, as nothing more than steps. If you can memorize the steps, you can do the problem. I was never going to be fast at completing math problems, but Mrs. Ells seemed to be okay with that. As long as I was trying, she gave me reinforcement. Thanks to her high expectations and willingness to teach and reteach, I saw my first success in math in many years.

Though she probably never intended that I visit her before school, during school, and after school—there I was. As she prepared for her day, she would find me pacing outside her door with a frantic question about the previous day's homework. Any question left unanswered from the day before made me lose sleep and rise early. As compulsive as hand washing, these thoughts dogged me until I could see Mrs. Ells. In all honesty the constant need for attention from Mrs. Ells was as much about understanding the material as it was about getting encouragement. It was like refueling in Miss Derek's class all over again. Thankfully Mrs. Ells didn't mind the constant interruptions. Well, if she did, she hid it well.

Mr. Parcin, my language arts and social studies teacher, was tall and had two-toned hair, a fact not lost on a girl vacillating between platinum and silver. He was stately and walked with nearly perfect posture, but for a slight hint of being pigeon-toed. This gave him an interesting gait. He talked like Vincent Price and dragged out certain words, giving him such a dramatic and flamboyant flair that even the mundane subject of book reports seemed exotic.

It was common for kids to be a little scared of Mr. Parcin. They had the right to be. He took his subject matter so seriously that if we didn't delight in doing our social studies assignment, he actually took it personally. He was known for small outbursts when students deserved it, and I came to view him as a passionate artist who suffered personally when we were frivolous with our homework.

Every once in a while he would open his eyes wide and say overly dramatic things such as, "Shari, if you don't get out your pencil and begin writing, we will all expire into a puddle on the floor." I thought this was just fantastic and kooky, and it made me sit forward and tune in.

I walked into his class the first day, tardy and carrying a disheveled book bag. He closed one eye, cocked his head, and held his hands on either side of his face. Apparently this was his look of disapproval. I didn't get it, though. After trying to be subtle, his warnings escalated and became more frequent. I think his exact words were, "Miss Rusch, we arrive on time, we have what we need to do our work with us, and we don't make excuses." *Did he talk to Mrs. Ells?* I wondered.

Seeing my newly organized binder brought cheers from Mr. Parcin. In honor of the occasion he gave me a pencil pouch and an eraser.

As if echoing Mrs. Ells, Mr. Parcin was convinced I could learn. Determined not to lose me, he presented material in a way I understood and made sure I had plenty of opportunities to ask questions.

Gaining confidence from his belief in me, I set out to do the impossible. I was going to conquer something Mr. Parcin liked to call *vocabulary words.* Up to this point I had only heard of spelling words. I soon learned that *vocabulary* was just the 10-dollar word for spelling and was designed to intimidate seventh graders.

Our assignment involved learning not only how to spell the words, but their definitions and how each could be used in a sentence. Applying myself very little to the first two vocabulary lessons got me a big fat zero. Careful not to humiliate me, Mr. Parcin took me aside after class one day and suggested that whatever method I was using to study wasn't exactly working.

I confided in him that I didn't actually have a method. Er . . .

um . . . in fact, I didn't actually study because I didn't know how.

Admitting that I wasn't good at studying was bold for me, but I put it out there just in case it would prevent me from having to do any more vocabulary assignments. No such luck. The next day Mr. Parcin gave me a stack of cards. On each card was a vocabulary word. On the back of each card were the definition and the word used in a sentence. Some gift. Mr. Parcin tapped on the top of the stack of cards and said, "These are flash cards. Read the word, say it out loud, spell it out loud, turn the card over, and read the definition and the word in a sentence. You do that lots of times throughout the week and by Friday you will do a lot better on the test." He was right.

Taking Mr. Parcin's advice I holed up in my room running my flash cards. It was kind of like learning the states and the capitals. This time, though, I was actually learning how to spell the words. Employing the same strategy I used with my United States puzzle, I had to take pictures in my mind and see the words with my eyes closed.

After studying with flash cards I saw success on the first test. I had to refine my strategy, though, because even with lots of repetition, I still managed to mix up letters and spell words wrong. I added writing the words over and over again to my study plan, and that seemed to help a lot. Test anxiety aside, I was able to see remarkable improvement in my vocabulary grade just from the beginning of the year. Even more dramatic was the difference in spelling grades from fifth and sixth grades. While never one to overdo, Mr. Parcin made it clear that he was impressed with my work. Every bit of attention he gave me made me want to work that much harder the next week.

Soon, I was applying the use of flash cards and other successful strategies to every class. When I saw a slight bit of success, I added a new strategy and tested the results. It was a bit hit-and-miss, but eventually, I had a sort of playbook of what worked for me. While this sounds good, it took a lot of energy. It wasn't long before I was pushing myself so hard that I got kind of off balance.

With little need for sleep and a bent toward compulsivity, I allowed my study time to take on a rigid shape. What started as a whim motivated by inspiring teachers became a rigid set of rules and requirements.

When I came home from school, I would run around our neighborhood until my mom returned from work. Once she was home, I would hide out in my bedroom until all hours studying. My studying was ordered from easiest to hardest assignment. I knew I needed to see some progress or I would get frustrated. I made homework a game by telling myself all I had to do was one assignment and then I could quit. After a quick break, I would come back and do the next assignment, still telling myself I'd only need to do one assignment. Suddenly the daunting task of five assignments was down to three and the mountain was whittled to doable. It was a trick of the mind, but it got me past quitting right at the start.

I'd like to say that all of my assignments were done with great care. Well, the truth is I rushed through a lot of work because my attention span was short and my ability to sit was even shorter. I hurried through assignments before I lost focus. I couldn't interrupt an assignment and come back to it (harkening back to what happened when I was interrupted while doing dishes). If I returned to it after leaving it undone, I became uncomfortable and uneasy. It was like I didn't know how to start in the middle or couldn't remember exactly what to do. This situation improved over time, but in the beginning I just gave myself a pass for turning in so-so work and felt good about accomplishing anything at all.

Saving the hardest assignment until the end of a long work session (or group of sessions) was not necessarily the right thing to do. Often I was so burned out on studying that the hardest assignment never was completed. To be honest this usually meant that math, science, or French was left on the cutting-room floor. I had no teacher willing to accept excuses, so in time I learned to push myself to refuel with food, water, and/or exercise so I could keep going. In some cases I actually got up even earlier in the morning to complete unfinished work. I became used to living on four hours of sleep.

Even though I struggled with writing, Mr. Parcin encouraged me to keep trying. No doubt he was one of many who had a hard time deciphering what I was trying to say. Always giving me the benefit of the doubt, he offered constructive suggestions about how to make my writing clear and gave me templates for how to write a sentence, a paragraph, and an essay.

Thanks to Mr. Parcin's willingness to overlook obvious issues, I didn't fall in love with writing, but I was less afraid of it. Previously, teachers were so busy correcting structural problems they didn't stop to see that I actually had some good ideas. With my papers covered in red ink I would become resistant and eventually quit. Following Mr. Parcin's lead, other teachers explained they would be willing to overlook some penmanship, spelling, grammar, and word usage issues to concentrate on content (what I was saying). Their support helped me stay motivated.

A DIFFICULT BUT USEFUL LESSON

With a tremendous amount of assistance from my teachers I entered the home stretch of the first quarter looking forward to seeing one of the best report cards ever. As the end of the quarter drew near, though, I began to get tired. I was living on little sleep, a challenge even for a hyperactive person. I had to work so hard and spend so much time studying, there just weren't enough hours in the day. My homework sessions were unforgiving. Implementing suggested practices including flash cards, tape recorders (a family member reading books onto tape), and combining senses (write/see, say/see) into a plan of attack, I pushed myself to the limit. Battling internal and external distractions and compulsions left me totally spent. Tired and on edge, I was about to make a terrible mistake.

Frazzled after another long night of studying, I botched a vocabulary test. Having come so far, I did not want to fail. We were told to exchange papers for grading. Instead I kept my paper and corrected several words that would have otherwise caused me to get a failing grade.

I left the class with a heavy heart. I knew I had done a very wrong thing. I was convicted, but afraid to tell on myself; someone in our class did it for me. Mr. Parcin confronted our class. He could have called me on the carpet; instead, he left it up to my conscience to compel me to confess. Two other students came forward. Apparently I wasn't the only one who had corrected his or her own paper. I waited until everyone left the classroom and fell apart. I apologized profusely and said I would never do it again. All Mr. Parcin said was, "I am disappointed in you." That was all that needed to be said. My mentor thought less of me. There could be no greater punishment.

Pushing On

Seeing B's and C's on my report card should have made me happy. There was no time for celebration, though. My only reaction was, *I could have done better.* With the compulsiveness usually devoted to washing my hands, I went headlong into a stepped-up study regimen.

My game plan written, I went to work. I was rarely free, and my usual playtime after school was enveloped by studying. With only brief breaks for respite, I fell into a rhythm. My last report card had brought accolades and even shock from my family members, but with all the distractions in our lives, I felt I had to make more of an impact. I did not have an exact goal in mind, just to do better.

Somewhere beneath the surface I thought, *If I get good grades, I can make our lives better.*

By semester's end I had a 4.0 GPA. That was only the second report card of my life I hadn't wanted to put through the wash to make it unreadable. I may have had to do every extra-credit project in the history of my school, but if life had a pinnacle, this was mine. My mom gave me a big hug and told me how proud she was of me. My grandmother did not want to allow this moment to go unrecognized, so she had a trophy made for me with an inscription describing my accomplishment with year and date.

I had dreamed of a day when I would not be an embarrassment. This was it. The strange thing is, instead of feeling fulfilled, I could only look toward my next report card. It was as if I had made it to the summit of the mountain but not the peak. I was tired but willing to keep going. The question was how I would go about keeping the grades. The work was only going to get harder. I leaned in with my shoulder to the wheel hoping one more good report card would change everything.

GIVING IT AWAY

In some sort of strange effort to right the wrongs of the previous year, I went back to my sixth-grade classroom. Giving Mr. Boise the benefit of the doubt, I hoped that if I shared my report card with him, he would apologize for taking away Cali and making me feel small. When I walked into his classroom he didn't seem the least bit glad or surprised to see me. I told him I had some good news. I held out my report card, but he continued shuffling papers on his desk. "Here," I said, handing him the well-worn paper. He barely looked up.

I said, "Mr. Boise, I got straight A's. I really did it." Still no comment. I put my report card in my pocket and walked home.

It was one of many moments I gave away something important to me saying, "Please like me. If I do this, will you like me?" Nike tennis shoes or a 4.0—so hard fought and so easily diminished by a distant stranger or would-be friend.

No Turning Back

Just days after I received my 4.0, my sister and I were taken from class and told there was a family emergency. We were picked up by the mother of one of Shawn's friends and taken to their home. Uncertain about the nature of the emergency, my sister and I were very scared. After two hours my mom arrived to pick us up. She was very pale and her hands were shaking. She sat down with my sister and me and told us that Lisa had tried to kill herself and was on life support.

Apparently, after coming home from school Lisa had gotten into an argument with her father on the phone. It seems Bill had learned of possible drug use or other activity and said that they would talk about it when he got home. Upset by her own behavior and the ramifications of her actions, she went into the garage, stood on her motorcycle, and put my dog's chain around her neck. My mom had spoken on the phone with Lisa and could tell she was very upset. She left work early and hurried home.

We will never know if the kickstand on the motorcycle went out accidentally or if Lisa jumped. We will never know if Lisa hoped my mom would get there in time to save her and this was all just a cry for help. Unfortunately, my mom arrived on the scene too late. Mom made every attempt to get Lisa down, but she was already unconscious. By the time the ambulance reached the hospital, she had slipped into a coma.

She died three days later.

If home was a difficult place to live in before, it became unbearable. Bill was inconsolable and volatile. There was fear that he would do something to harm himself or others. Though my mom was completely shattered, she was levelheaded enough to see the seriousness of the situation. My grandparents offered us an opportunity to stay with them, but neither Shawn nor I wanted to be too far away from our mom. We opted for the safety of school during the day and went to friends' houses during the evening.

I tried to hold my head up during the day so my mom wouldn't see me cry. She had enough to deal with, but I was beyond devastated. At night I sobbed uncontrollably. The girl who was like me—learning disabilities and all—was never coming back. I moved forward feeling a terrible sense of guilt and felt sure I could have said or done something to save her. Second-guessing myself was constant. I was carrying the weight of the world on my thin, frail shoulders.

Lisa's memorial overflowed with people. Everyone appeared to be in shock and terribly sad. Seeing the finality of her death and realizing that people might forget her, or worse, remember her suicide but not her name, truly shook me. I thank God that instead of seeing her act of suicide as something romantic, I saw it for the horror it was. I knew that no matter how dark things became, I would never do what she did. I wanted to live, I just didn't know how. Even with a diminished sense of my value, I determined that as long as there was breath in my body, I would keep going.

Running Away

Every day after Lisa's death only ensured that Bill would be more irrational and out of control. We grew more and more afraid of him. On many occasions he told me, "You look so much like Lisa. Now that she is gone, you can take her place." Being a little bit older now, I had learned of past abuses against Lisa. I did not want to take her place. I came home only to sleep, but I blocked my door with a chair.

Bill had now been out of work for a year. Any resources my mom had when she entered the marriage were totally depleted, and our finances were in disarray. An independent show producer, my mom was unable to generate enough money to support our family; she knew we needed steady income. Though a job as assistant manager of a new mall was well out of the area of her expertise and required significant marketing experience, my mom applied for the position. By the grace of God she got it. Unexpectedly, my grandparents' rental house, which was located near the mall where my mom was going to work, became available.

As our home situation worsened by the day, my mom viewed her new job and place to live as the security we needed to escape from Bill.

On a day when we knew Bill was going to be away from our home, we loaded a truck and ran away.

10

Another New Life

We moved thirty miles from our previous residence, but you would have thought we were standing still. Everything had changed, but nothing had changed. Our living situation was safer, but we were not better prepared to cope or make good decisions. The only thing I knew for sure was that I wanted to fit in. Having realized that a year's worth of good grades was not enough to ensure happiness, I started searching for more. I felt sure I would be happy if only I _____ (fill in the blank with any manner and form of empty pursuits and you will have the story of my life for the next five years).

Though I was 13 years old, I was the same little girl wishing for acceptance on the playground; it's just that the stakes had been raised. Two years earlier I believed that if I got good grades, I could make my mom happy and bring my dad back home. It didn't take long to see that getting good grades was not enough to accomplish either of these goals. Good, but not enough. Now I carried all the guilt and shame over the loss of my stepsister and the life we had just left behind. Additional baggage simply served to add to my motivation to run as fast as I could to better myself. I was sure that if I improved myself, I could make up for everything and find acceptance.

"If only" were the two most common words in my vocabulary. *If only* I could be more, *if only* I could be smarter, *if only* I could be better. All my goals and dreams were wrapped up in "if only." Everything depended on my elevating myself. My current and future happiness depended on whether I could please others (Dad, Mom, family, friends, etc.). This would involve achieving enough academically and socially to reach a certain level, but it was unclear what level that was. When everything depends on acceptance, and acceptance is conditional (clothes, shoes, hair, grades, awards, banners, positions on squads, teams, or within certain groups), you spend a lot of time contorting yourself. Because you don't like yourself to begin with, there is really nothing anyone else can do to give you acceptance. It's a vicious cycle for sure.

There it is, in a nutshell. I didn't like myself. Until I understood the truth of this and did something about it, I would spend a lot of time trying to cover scars with superficial means: clothes, makeup, awards—any quick fix would do.

Years of being called names left me feeling I was nothing short of hideous. I thought, *If I can only look better when I go to my new school, and get good grades, it will change my life.* Right? Sure I was such a tough case that nothing short of a miracle, time travel, or plastic surgery would help, I did my best to address problem areas.

Did I mention I had platinum hair? First order of business—change my hair color to something actually found in nature. Then I decided to straighten the curly mess. This process took over an hour and a half each day and involved a high-wattage hair dryer and all kinds of straightening gadgets. The result was not spectacular but better than braids tightly crossing the top of my head. Yes, I actually once wore my hair like a Dutch milk-maid. I have no idea why. For eighth grade, this had to go.

I also worked hard to stop squinting, even though my hard contacts often felt like sandpaper in my eyes. I was semi-successful at this. My expression changed from a continual look of extreme concern to appearing only slightly irritated.

I knew that to really do things right I had to wear different clothes. With a few odd jobs as my source of income, I did the best I could, going coatless in winter and buying summer items on sale at the end of the season.

Trying to stand straight at the bus stop, I shivered in the cold. I looked more like I should be going on a tropical vacation, not to school. Based on my light outfits, a rumor soon began that I was from California and my parents were rich. When I learned of the story that was circulating, I made no effort to correct it. If people wanted to say I was rich and from California, I was totally cool with that. It beat the real story by a mile. I figured people would learn eventually that I lived in a rental house featuring moss-green carpet, discolored linoleum, and furniture from a secondhand store. For the moment I was happy to be from LA.

At the time I didn't realize how this made-up story would color people's view of me. I was a new girl, wearing "California" clothes, with rich parents. This image went over like a lead balloon. And while I was just trying to keep my past a secret, my quietness and unintentionally irritated expression (due to painful contact lenses) led people to believe I was stuck-up. I mistakenly thought I would have at least a few days before people started hating me. No such luck.

What a turnaround, though. I didn't lisp or stutter. I wore normal clothes (if normal is summer clothes in winter). I had a 4.0 and went to honors classes. Oh, and I "lived in a mansion with my rich parents from California." People who would have once put me down or shunned me for being slow and odd-looking now shunned me for having it so good. What was going on here?

Since I might not have the one friend I longed for because I was now "too much," I was willing to hide behind the façade. The idealized version of me didn't get up at 4:00 A.M. to straighten my hair and study. This girl didn't have a stepsister who killed herself or a mother who drank too much. No one knew I had nightmares every night and was afraid most of the time. No one knew this girl who seemed to have it easy struggled with just about everything except cleaning. I hid my past well and shouldered rejection for being "too much." Stuffing everything would soon result in stomach pain so severe it could not be ignored, and I gobbled antacids, refusing to acknowledge how hiding my true self was making me sick.

I wasn't the only one with some sort of ailment. Everyone in my family had become sick. My mom was working long hours with a boss who was, to put it mildly, not very nice. She quickly developed a variety of stress-related illnesses and was sick often. Within weeks of the school year's start, my sister came down with mononucleosis so severe that she could not raise her head. Along with my ulcer, I began showing some semblance of my sister's illness. My glands were swelling in my neck so much that my face actually changed shape. I was almost always fatigued.

Teachers Save the Day Once Again

While I was an outcast socially for wearing summer clothes and looking aloof, I could not have asked for better teachers at my new school. Mrs. Moden, my math teacher, was a stout woman with a big voice. It was not unlike her to yell like a short-order cook, "Get out your homework assignments before I flunk all of you." She was joking. I took it seriously and cowered in the back row. I was so intimidated by her that I let go of some of my dogged efforts to keep up, and soon my grade was in jeopardy. I didn't raise my hand and was afraid to approach her desk for extra help. When my first few assignments didn't look so good, I think she thought I was a highly organized goof-off.

I could tell she was getting frustrated with me, and I was worried about my grade—so worried I decided to do the unthinkable and tell the truth. I took her aside after class and whispered in hushed tones, "Mrs. Moden, I have dyslexia and that is why—"

She interrupted me. "Don't use that as an excuse." It really hurt my feelings. She saw the look on my face, and I could tell she immediately regretted her words. She may have thought my many questions were generated because I was daydreaming, but the exact opposite was true. I was fighting to pay attention and even so couldn't understand what was being said. The very next day she told me she knew I was not making up excuses and offered whatever help I needed to succeed. We became fast friends. Now when she yelled at everyone, I got the joke.

Though Mrs. Glode might not have known it, she was my best friend. I had her for honors English and social studies. She was a very nice person and a good teacher, easygoing but with high expectations. I was honored to be in her honors classes but scared to death all at once. How would I keep up? I never confided in her that I had learning issues, but no doubt the furious note taking and repetitive questions gave me away. All you had to do was look at my handwriting to glimpse the problem. Once again, I was dumbfounded that I was in higher-level English, considering I couldn't spell simple words like *which* correctly. With subdued humor and endless patience, Mrs. Glode helped me with repetition, reteaching, templates, and other accommodations so no one would ever know my secret.

Oh, the many days I spent in her classroom during lunchtime. No wonder she was so thin; she never got to eat. I found myself so overwhelmed with the noise in the lunchroom that I pretended I had an assignment to do so I could hide in Mrs. Glode's room. She never complained but no doubt wished for a few minutes to herself.

At night I often came home to an empty house. After cleaning to put my brain in order, I studied until all hours. My homework regimen was very strict but allowed for frequent breaks for water or snacks. If interrupted, I was now able to return to assignments and complete them. This was a big step from the previous year. The challenge I faced every day was retaining information. It was a weird kind of short-term memory erosion. I would learn something; then it was gone. So often I would study material repetitively before I went to bed. While I was trying to go to sleep, I would close my eyes and try to see the material again. Sometimes when I woke up, the information was still there—or at least part of it. This practice was just another version of "mind pictures." If I could re-create a picture of the information with my eyes closed, I could often retain it.

In time I would learn other tricks, like not to panic on the first day. I felt sick in each new class. Like clockwork, a stomachache would hit. No doubt my ulcer and a sinking feeling collided when I looked at each syllabus. *How am I going to do this?* I would ask myself. Fear would pour over me like cold water. Then I would stiffen my back in my chair and prepare for battle. I would tell myself every time, "You have felt this before. You have been afraid before. This is the same fear. It will go away. The panic will settle. You can do this thing. More flash cards, more remedial help—that is all you need. You can do this thing."

My method was unorthodox. It was called "whatever worked." While bouncing my knee under the desk at school, I quickly and efficiently organized my book bag and all the items on my desk. Then, just as quickly, I would fully label my paper and try to take organized notes. Before leaving class I would take my notes to my teachers and try to fill in parts I missed. During lunch I would work on homework, so that if I had trouble, I could get help at school. Arriving early at school provided another opportunity to ask for help with my homework. With few distractions in my social life, it was easy to keep pushing.

One 4.0, then another. It appeared that my system was working.

The Happiest Cheerleader in the World

By the middle of the year I actually had a couple of really nice friends. No one was able to get too close to me, but visiting my home dispelled any myth that we were well off. Even with some acceptance I still felt inadequate. There was an emptiness that couldn't be filled. Call it silly, call it shallow, but for a long time I had the idea that if I became a cheerleader, I would always be happy. Aren't all cheerleaders happy? (Don't answer that question.) I was pretty sure that if I became a cheerleader, the sting of being called "retard" would suddenly disappear. Not deterred by lackluster coordination skills, I prepared for spring semester with one goal in mind—to try out.

Returning from spring break I could not overcome a terrible sore throat and an overwhelming feeling of fatigue. Sure that it was caused by too many late nights studying, I didn't tell my mom about it. I soon was too weak to walk. Within days I was hospitalized with viral pneumonia.

Frighteningly thin because I was too sick to eat and battling a raging fever, I struggled to even lift my limbs. Though in terrible physical pain, I tried to will myself well.

I finally made it home from the hospital but could barely get out of bed. It was clear I wasn't going back to school anytime soon. Cheerleading tryouts took place without me. This shouldn't have been earth-shattering, but for some reason it was. I fell into a deep despair and could not stop crying. I thought I was crying about not being a cheerleader. I think I was actually crying for all the losses that had taken place over the years. I was crying about real fears and imagined fears. I was crying from a very deep well. As soon as my mom left for work, I started crying and didn't stop until she got home. This went on for several weeks.

I wish I had known then how to put everything into perspective. I was just too young. I had God, I loved Him, but I was very weak. I didn't allow Him to take over. I tried to strong-arm the situation by praying to Him and then doing my own thing. So the race continued as I looked for ways to gain acceptance. No matter how much I got, though, it was never enough.

When I returned to school, I was emaciated and weak. This was the perfect time to run for school president, don't you think? I know, I know. It just doesn't make any sense. I was relatively new at the school. Who was going to vote for me anyway? Once again searching for acceptance and a way to fill the deep hole in my soul, I was grasping at straws. I didn't make it past the primary.

A good lesson could have been learned here, but the only

thing my lackluster performance in the election did was to intensify my resolve to be more.

Finishing school with a solid 4.0, I planned to do even better the next year. How you do better than straight A's, I don't know, but I was determined to. I spent the next three months trying to figure out how.

11

Time Misspent

Searching for acceptance in all the wrong places, I tried all kinds of silly things to get attention. I spent a lot of time going in the wrong direction. So busy trying to achieve popularity or notoriety, I neglected to realize that I had much to be proud of. In the end, the void I was trying to fill with superficial endeavors would remain empty until I faced the source of my pain.

I finished eighth grade feeling lost. I had missed cheerleading tryouts and wouldn't have another chance until I reached high school. As I started ninth grade, I searched for other opportunities to find acceptance. Apparently, studying 12 hours a day was not enough to keep me occupied. My deep-seated need for acceptance led to my next step toward distinction: getting a letterman's jacket—with a letter on it no less. Did I mention I was uncoordinated?

Having taken only a few hula lessons as a child, and barely able to execute a cartwheel, I followed a friend's advice to try out for gymnastics. What? Being completely delusional I decided I would. Thankfully the coaches opted not to cut anyone from the team or I would have been the first to go. I expected I'd never be in a meet, and I was under the mistaken impression that I would get a letter for having participated. Oh, you actually have to compete to get a letter? Well, there goes my plan.

Never a quitter, I stayed on the team and even substituted as an exhibition competitor (you get a score, but it's not counted) for an injured teammate at a competition. When several injured gymnasts were taken off the roster, I was asked as a last resort. Due to bad eyesight and questionable coordination, I fell off the beam several times. One such fall resulted in a near-death experience with my head narrowly missing the beam. I had the lowest score of the meet and felt grateful it was an away event. Hoping never to have to compete again, I "accidentally" jumped from the beam onto a spotting block at a practice and sprained my ankle. I was gratefully placed on the injured list and finished the season hobbling all the way.

This experience could be placed in the same category as running for president of my school. Why did I do things that were so out of reach? I mean really, shouldn't you at least be able to do a forward roll if you are going to become a gymnast? And furthermore, you should know better than to miss a month of school with a serious illness and return to run for a major office. My discernment was really in question.

I was disappointed in my decision making and vowed to regroup. I wish I could have, but I was on a crash course. I had so much to be thankful for, but I saw the glass as half empty.

I looked totally normal as I walked down the school hall-
ways, but I was a hollow girl. Teachers could probably see that
my tireless effort to get A's in every one of my classes, even those
that were pass-fail, was emanating from something more than
the need to please. No doubt even a few of my classmates wondered what was driving me. Smiling all the way, but totally
guarded, I made sure everyone stayed at a distance for fear they
would learn my secrets. I laughed at all the jokes (even though I
didn't get them) and went along like I fit right in. I might be
surrounded by people, but I felt totally alone.

No doubt my home life didn't help with my insecurities. My
mom was very ill. She had lost weight (a good thing on its face),
but had done so with the help of two serious stress-related intes-
tinal illnesses. A heavy work schedule and chronic illness left her
gaunt and tired. Unable to rest, she took sleeping aids to chase
away thoughts of Lisa. That would eventually lead to other medi-
cations and increasing alcohol use. She never looked out of control or was unable to do her work, but she wasn't happy. I
became accustomed to throwing away various-sized bottles and
their contents whenever possible. Using "cleaning house" as a
cover, I became complicit in her addiction. Instead of con-
fronting the situation, I just got rid of the evidence.

A new man had entered her life. Jackson was a nice person,
but not much on kids. While I tagged along at times, I did not
feel particularly welcome. When I had wanted Mom to leave
Bill, I had a picture in my mind of how things would be. This
was definitely not it.

My prayers at night were no longer filled with hope, just

desperation. *Where is the God of my childhood?* I wondered. I used to feel very close to Him; now I just found myself pleading. I began to assign human characteristics to Him. God, just like everyone else, couldn't love me unless I was more. I began to say, "God will love me when—" According to me there was no end to the list of things I would need to become to gain His acceptance.

And the Most Unlikely Cheerleader Is?

Sure God had heard my prayers, I learned that ninth graders would have a chance to try out for JV cheer squad at the high school. Can everybody say, "Yea!"? Is it just me, or does this sound kind of unimportant? While it wasn't world peace, when you have a low self-concept, it can seem really close. As if I were preparing for the national homework speed trials, I took every bit of enthusiasm, energy, and determination I had and applied it all to learning how to deliver a cheer. One problem, some cheers actually involved spelling. "Give me a—" *Well, this is going to be a problem,* I thought.

At tryouts I looked like I had two left feet and several arms. I had no idea what I was doing. My sister, on the varsity squad at the time, quickly bowed out of teaching the routines because she didn't want to appear biased. Let's be honest; she didn't want to watch me spell our school name backward. I looked like an octopus trying to knit—seriously goofy.

The friend who attended the tryout practice with me decided to rescue me from myself. She broke down every move into smaller parts. She stood behind me and moved my arms while I looked into a window at my reflection. Again and again we would go through the moves like physical flash cards. When she went home after a long rehearsal, I continued drilling the movements. It felt like I was trying to speak a foreign language with my body, but I was determined to not give up. There were many long nights of rehearsing followed by a relentless homework schedule. Even dark circles under my eyes and a few pulled muscles would not deter me. For my own good I should have given up, but I was either too stubborn or too stupid to let it go.

Thanks to my tireless partner willing to go to great lengths to help her dyslexic friend turn the right way, a very peppy dance she choreographed to a song called "Groove Line," and extremely low turnout, I actually made the JV squad. I would begin tenth grade as a cheerleader.

I was very excited for about five minutes. Then I realized that while I had tried out with one cheer and one short dance, I now was going to need to learn about 50 cheers and dances. Uh-oh!

After I made the cheer squad, I paused and waited. Then I waited some more. I spent the rest of that day waiting. Still it didn't come. I was sure any minute my self-esteem was going to show up. Isn't that what a cheer sweater gets you? I mistakenly thought so. When self-esteem didn't show up, I thought I would give it a little more time. It was just hiding somewhere.

While I waited for popularity to arrive, I prepared for the end of ninth grade. One of the culminating activities was an event called the Ninth-Grade Party. This event included a dance and award ceremony where I was crowned Miss Kenmore. No, I was not the queen of a Sears brand of home appliances. Miss

Kenmore was a "distinguished" title given to the most popular ninth-grade girl at Kenmore Junior High. Well, the truth is, I was kind of just half Miss Kenmore, because I tied with another girl. Being half of something isn't all it's cracked up to be, by the way. I told myself that if I had been a real achiever I would have gotten the whole Miss Kenmore title. I really knew how to put a damper on things. I had been waiting for acceptance and there it was all the time. Too bad I didn't notice it.

Ironically, I also tied for the position of highest academic honors in my ninth-grade class. The boy I tied with was actually brilliant, which made me question how I had the same grade point average as he did, but I was honored when each of us was asked to deliver a speech at the ceremony at the end of the year. After the honor thing wore off I started to realize what I had agreed to. I was going to say something in front of a large group of people? How did I say yes to this? My mom saw that I had gone from nervous to petrified in a matter of days. While she tried to offer support, nothing she said could diminish my dread.

The speech was to be just a few sentences. You would have thought it was a State of the Union address. When the day finally arrived, I could barely walk or even stand because my legs were so wobbly. Holding on to walls as we walked into our cafeteria, the girl who didn't sweat had drops of perspiration coming out of her hair. I saw my mom on the way into the cafeteria (sitting in the front row, of course) and mouthed the words, "Help me!" She smiled as if to reassure me, but it didn't cover the fact that she was wringing her hands.

I was glad to be able to sit down, but being on stage facing everyone made me so unsteady I didn't think I would be able to get up again. I nearly fainted when my name was announced and I had to walk to the podium.

My whole intention with this speech was to thank my teachers for their support. Suddenly, at the crucial moment in the speech when I was going to list their names, I couldn't remember any of them. I looked down at my notes hoping for something to click. I looked behind me at my teachers, the ones I knew well, as they sat in a row on the stage. Nothing! I turned back toward the audience as waves of panic came over me.

I knew I couldn't read under pressure, which is why I had memorized my speech. Well, all except for the names of my teachers. I hadn't memorized my teachers' names because, well, I didn't think I would forget them. Oops!

"I would like to thank my teachers . . ." long pause, "um, er, um . . ." My mom knew I was struggling and began praying my brain would unfreeze. Throwing out a lifeline she mouthed the words, "Mrs. Glode."

I thought she said, "Middle lobe," and my heart began to race. *What does "middle lobe" have to do with anything?* I thought, frantically searching my mind for a connection.

More time passed. The music to *Jeopardy* was playing loudly in my head. Suddenly the words her lips were forming made a connection and I blurted out, "Glode!" Pause, "um, er . . . I would like to thank Mrs. Glode." As if they had never left, all the names of my teachers suddenly slipped back into my mind. I quickly rattled them off before they escaped again. With a huge sigh of relief my mom slumped in her chair.

I was so relieved to turn the microphone over to the smart kid I had tied with, I nearly ran to my seat. "It" was over. As I wiped the sweat from my brow, I was determined to never do any form of public speaking ever again.

No doubt all my teachers were sorry to see me go (just kidding). I'm sure they all took a nap when I left. When you are high octane like me, always pushing yourself a little too hard, you tend to push people around you too. My teachers were probably tired of seeing me outside the teachers' lounge during their lunch period waiting to ask the same question for the fiftieth time. No doubt they found peace when I headed to high school.

DIRECTIONALLY CHALLENGED

The summer before tenth grade I got a job at the mall where my mom worked. I had a highly sought-after position working at the information desk. I rented strollers and collected lost items. I also was the individual patrons came to for directions. Let's get this straight. I had no sense of direction and could not tell right from left, but I was in charge of giving people directions. Clearly my mom, the assistant manager, had paid someone off. I wore a lovely yellow suit and unintentionally told everyone how to get to the wrong store.

Replicate that "success" and you have my cheerleading experience in a nutshell. I practiced all summer with a lovely group of girls who were just coming to terms with the fact that I had brain damage. Touching my hair and pretending I was a dumb blonde was better than admitting to oxygen deprivation at birth.

It was like having all of my limbs plugged in separately. Ever try patting your head and rubbing your stomach? Well, multiply that awkward feeling by a thousand and that is pretty much where we were.

After relentless practice sessions I managed to learn most of the cheers and dances that our squad required. I say "most" because there were certain routines that refused to stick. I was placed in the back of formations for those selections and crossed my fingers that I wouldn't embarrass myself or others if my brain suddenly glitched. All in all, cheerleading went well through tenth grade. I only yelled "first and ten" at a soccer game once.

KEEPING THINGS IN BOXES

My sister and I had the same cheer advisor, Rod Pressey. He was actually an award-winning basketball coach but had taken over for the cheer advisor when she resigned. No one volunteered to take the job so he was stuck until a replacement came to save him. Though my sister and I had stayed clear of my mom's dating situation so far, we remained skeptical of her choices. Taking matters into her own hands Shawn arranged for several "chance" meetings between my mom and Mr. Pressey. Within a year they were married. My sister and I were really happy for them, but we kept all of our belongings in boxes just in case it didn't work out.

Though I did want my mom to be happy I had an ulterior motive for wanting her to get together with Mr. Pressey: He had a master's degree in math and I was currently having a terrible time (massive understatement) in tenth-grade geometry.

GEOMETRY AND OTHER SUBJECTS
THAT DON'T MAKE SENSE

It wasn't too hard to see why I was having trouble with geometry. First of all, it's a subject that requires "spatial sense"—of which I had none. Also, I had a teacher who was a genius, and well, I wasn't. All of the really smart kids in my class would nod their heads when he would explain a concept, and I would think, *Should I be nodding my head? Why is everyone nodding their heads? The man is speaking another language and they are all nodding their heads. What is going on here?*

Even with Rod's help I finished my first semester in geometry with a resounding thud. I got my first B in over three years. I would have liked to blame the evil genius teacher, though everyone else in his class seemed to get it but me. I was so crushed. It was like a major ding on my record. When other people responded, "Hey, it's just a B," I wanted to sock them right in the nose (in a Christian way, of course). Didn't everyone know that my grades were my identity? It was like someone had just amputated an important limb. A level of shame and embarrassment worthy only of a fallen world leader came over me. I was really out of control over this.

Barely holding myself together about my grade, which might as well have been an F in my opinion, I went to see my school counselor, Loret Spesher. Loret would see me through many things in the coming years. There was never anything earth-shattering, but in my fragile state everything was a big deal.

I was crying so hard that she couldn't understand me, and Loret did her best to offer support. When she finally realized I was cracking up over a B, she was perplexed. No doubt she too was wondering why this was a big deal. After sniffling and sobbing, I gained my composure and tried to explain the situation. Before I spoke, I closed the blinds on her window, closed the door to her office, and made her take a vow of secrecy regarding what she was about to hear. Thinking I was going to reveal something really devastating, I looked around as if checking for bugging devices and said, "I'm dyslexic and have trouble learning."

Loret tried not to smile. This was the big secret?

I went on, "Mrs. Spesher, I get up at three in the morning most days and go to bed late at night. I do lots of crazy things to get information in my head. I do all this so no one will ever know. I did everything I could to get an A in my math class. Either the subject is impossible or my teacher needs to teach me in another way. He is really smart, and I don't think he understands why I don't get what he is saying. All I know is that I need to switch classes."

Mrs. Spesher took a deep breath and collected her thoughts. I looked at her intently. She said, "Shari, thank you for sharing this with me." She then waved her hand in the air as if to erase my secrets. Continuing, she said, "I will take care of it." I believed her.

By the next day I was in another person's class. I did not get a B in math again.

Mrs. Spesher became a trusted friend and confidante. Just like many educators who came before, after meeting with me once, she too missed her lunch hour quite a few times. She was a good sport about it, though. I only bothered her if it was really important.

Terribly disturbed by what I felt was a failing grade, I was about to be dealt another blow to the ego. It was clear to Mr. Reston, my driver's education teacher, that I should probably never get behind the wheel of a car. With slow reflexes, no sense of direction, and lack of quick decision-making skills, I was quite literally an accident waiting to happen.

My teacher made every effort to keep me off the roads with elaborate excuses and reasons why I could only drive in empty parking lots. At first I bought his story about how my particular driving style didn't lend itself to two-lane roads, but soon it became clear that he was holding me back. I can't blame him really. No one in my family was ever willing to get into a car with me, either. The whole learner's permit concept of driving with your parents became null and void when the fear factor of letting me drive became too great.

Despite my limited experience behind the wheel, I graduated from driver's education and made plans to take my test. I passed the written exam with flying colors. The driving evaluation was another story. The tester said right and I went left. She said stop and I went right through a stop sign. When the fact that I had just run a stop sign sunk in, I stopped the car immediately—in the middle of a busy intersection. The lady evaluating me was now clutching her chest and the door handle. At that moment I pretty much knew it was over. I not only didn't get my license, the tester suggested I wait several months before trying again. I am not sure they're supposed to say things like that. But can you blame her?

I hung my head as we drove home from the DMV. I had told my friends I was going to get my license. Apparently, I thought I could drive. *Why didn't someone tell me the truth?* I wondered. I should have gathered this information from the stricken look on my driver's ed teacher's face. There were times, though, that I was too thick in the head to get the drift. By the time we got home, I had a story made up to cover the whole debacle. The next day at school when my friends asked if I got my license, I looked at them with all sincerity and said, "My blinker on our car broke, so I was unable to take the test." This was the best story that I could come up with? Here's the problem: People got a little suspicious when I didn't go back to take my test for nine months. I mean, how long does it take to fix a blinker?

I finally got my license and within days got into an accident. No one was hurt, but I did put a quick end to a neighbor's bumper. I guess I don't need to mention that the accident was my fault. Well, it was. From that time forward my driving privileges were curtailed.

HUGH WHO?

God often opened windows for me when a door was shut. In this case He opened a door and Wyatt Earp walked in. On the heels of winning the prize for driving like Mr. Magoo, I was told by one of my teachers that I had been nominated to go to the

Hugh O'Brien Leadership Conference. Wow, that's great! Um, who is Hugh O'Brien? I was so embarrassed. I didn't know that Mr. O'Brien had been a Hollywood actor and played Wyatt Earp, no less. I also didn't know that he had started a foundation to help young scholars learn about the free enterprise system. Okay, I am going to be honest. My first thought was, *How did I get nominated for this? I don't know what free enterprise is.* I thought free enterprise had to do with Star Trek. So I went to ask for counsel from Mrs. Spesher, who was not surprised to see me. Getting the drift by now that I pretty much worried about everything, she was just waiting for me to show up.

Mrs. Spesher explained that I had been nominated to go to a three-day conference during spring break. I would have a chance to hear outstanding speakers on the topic of, you guessed it, free enterprise. She told me there would be all kinds of wonderful activities and events and even a dance. After she was done, I hesitated for a minute and said, "But I don't even know what free enterprise is."

Mrs. Spesher thought I was kidding. What 4.0 student doesn't know what free enterprise is? She laughed and said, "Shari, you are going to have a great time."

After a lot of pressure from my family, I decided to go but worried about it every minute of the day until I arrived at the conference center, clammy and nervous.

Turns out I should have been clammy. The whole conference was a competition. At the end of the weekend one person was going to get picked to go to the Hugh O'Brien Nationals, which upon my arrival I knew nothing about. I think there may have even been an international competition too. Did I mention I didn't know what free enterprise was? *What am I doing here?* I wondered.

I would like to tell you that my knowledge of free enterprise made me Hugh's top gal, but I am afraid I did little to impress the judges during my stay. So why was this experience so great? I was surrounded by some truly outstanding young people, kids who were naturally smart. (I don't even think some of them had ever done extra credit, if you get my drift.) While I would have said I was totally out of my element, none of the other delegates seemed to think so. Their assumption was that if I was there, I was worthy. I was invited to sit with everyone at lunch, and people genuinely seemed interested in talking with me. I was absolutely sure I had never felt that level of acceptance.

Um, the truth is, I *had* felt that level of acceptance. At my school people liked me, but I didn't notice any of it. I was a numb girl who had yet to realize she fit in. I was so busy covering my supposed inadequacies that I didn't even feel the truth. I was no longer the outcast.

I didn't win a single award but left changed, if only for a moment. In tenth grade I had been a girl with a 4.0 GPA dating a guy who wasn't very nice to her. I was a cheerleader who was sad most of the time. I would head into eleventh grade and assume my position as the driven girl, but I was better for having seen how I was really viewed. If only I could have internalized the lesson and embraced how far God had brought me.

12

The Driven Girl

I had always hoped to erase the little girl that I was, but she refused to go quietly. Every cheerleading sweater I wore and every A I achieved was an attempt to get rid of any trace of my past. While I tried to run away from her, the little girl I used to be was the very source of any wisdom I carried. Her story, my story, was about God's plan being carried out regardless of what a standardized test or authority figure said. The battle with my past would rage on until I found a way to use it for good.

As I sat in the front of each class rigidly organizing my desktop with my tightly ordered book bag at my feet, I bordered on being irritating. When I ran flash cards continuously before school and asked repetitious questions of my teachers, no doubt at times I gave the wrong impression.

Did I mention that the stitch on the seam of my pants matched my shoelaces? When you appear to be bent on being perfect and are really, *really* intense, you don't always invite support. I know for a fact that some of my peers and teachers probably thought I was (to say the least) a head case. Most of them did not know, though, what I was running from or why I was hiding. Though I was not volunteering information, I wish there could have been more compassion for such a driven girl. I understand, though, why it was hard to get past my stressful exterior.

For every one of the people put off by my pushing, there were plenty who took it in stride and tried to help me. Take my typing teacher, for example. May God bless her. She tried every conventional way to teach me how to type. I just wasn't getting it. I typed everything backward. I would attempt to hit an A and hit the L on the opposite side of the keyboard—same finger position, but on the opposite side. If hand transplants were an option, I would likely have pursued one. Between dyslexia and coordination issues, it seemed hopeless.

Oh, did I mention I had ADHD? Putting me in a room filled with people typing and then asking me to do something meaningful is a surefire way to see me fail. I would get so wrapped up in the noise around me, I couldn't remember what I was supposed to be doing or how to do it.

After I made a rare tearful confession about my learning issues, my teacher decided to improvise. She took me out of our noisy room and let me sit alone in an empty room next door. She allowed me to teach myself using an instruction manual and did not require me to take timed tests. Eventually I got it. Well, sort of anyway. I was able to type letters but not numbers. Most of it was backward, but that is not important. Actually it is, but my point is I eventually learned a form of typing thanks to a teacher willing to find another way.

My typing teacher was just one of many teachers who helped me through my high school years. In ninth grade Mr. Halen helped me survive the early stages of Spanish. Regardless of the number of my missteps, he showed an unwavering belief in my ability to learn a second language. Mr. Rossen continued this process in following years, enabling me to go far beyond what anyone would have thought possible. Though I was never fluent in the language, I did learn to say, "Where's the bathroom?" which makes me ready for world travel. Did I mention I can say this phrase in French too?

The head coach of our varsity football team was also my biology teacher. He saw my intensity (which masked fear) but never got frustrated with my constant questions in his biology class. Having written "right" and "left" on players' shoes to help them go the right direction, Coach Cash was familiar with learning disabilities and sensitive to my situation. He was a great fit in terms of style for me, because he was methodical in his approach, breaking down complicated processes and concepts into smaller parts. In addition, he provided lots of visuals, offered supplementary written notes (to accompany my often sketchy in-class notes), and was available for help before, during, and after school.

In much the same way as Coach Cash, Mrs. Low and Mrs. Chaner saw me through Algebra 1 and Algebra 2, a feat worthy of medals. Even with Rod's help at home and two devoted teachers, I struggled at higher levels as math became more abstract.

Because of the dogged effort of my teachers and my motivation to get to college, I was able to accomplish much in a subject that, frankly, was beyond me. I finally quit math my senior year because of a little thing called "math analysis." I still regret this decision because I believe I disappointed Mrs. Low. I think she knew I was more worried about my grade point average than learning and viewed my quitting as a cop-out. I agree now, but at the time my GPA was my only ticket into college. I was afraid of failure and burned out. Quitting math was just one sign I was losing my momentum as high school neared its end.

Losing momentum at a crucial stage in the game was due to punishing discipline. I pushed myself too hard, then wondered why I collapsed. There were no rewards. If I got an A, I would be mad at myself that it wasn't an A+ and forge ahead toward that goal. Even after I had fully prepared for a test or quiz, I might bungle it. After a strong rebuke for my "careless" behavior, I would increase my study time and do every extra-credit project available to make up the difference. It was like a vendetta against my past. Don't just do better, do the best.

I was convinced I had to go above and beyond to prove my value. Case in point, to get into most colleges you needed three years of foreign language. I took five. Most colleges required three years of high school English. I took three and added college English just to make sure everyone knew I was serious. Oh, everyone knew I was serious, I'm sure. A girl unable to spell the word "which" correctly in any kind of consistent manner should definitely take an advanced placement course in English. First semester of my senior year I walked out of college English with my second B in high school. If people thought I cracked up over a B in geometry, they hadn't seen anything yet.

I cried to Mrs. Spesher. I cried to my teacher. I cried to a teacher who knew my teacher. I even cried to our new principal. He was a military man who looked a little stiff. Turns out, there was a really nice guy under his starched collar. Being new at the school, though, this was his first encounter with me. As I sobbed over my report card he looked unsure about what to do. When you usually deal with stoners and truants, a hysterical cheerleader can leave you speechless. At some point he said, "So, are you asking me to change the grade?"

"No," I said and sobbed some more. "I just, just, just (this is the part where my shoulders were heaving) want someone to understand."

He told me everything was going to be okay and escorted me out of his office before I asked for his hanky. A nice guy, but totally out of his element. I went home from school feeling my life might, in fact, be over.

My college-level English teacher took pity on me and gave me the opportunity to learn at a different pace, out of his classroom, on a pass-fail basis. I am sure he was just devastated to see me go (kidding). He offered me an opportunity to get credit in English by writing short stories. Those short stories eventually became the first draft of this book, by the way. Lemons into lemonade for sure. I took his offer and spent the rest of my senior year in the library during English class writing, something few could read due to spelling errors and inconsistent handwriting, but feeling good about the opportunity to put "my story" on paper.

Even with a new lease on college English, I was feeling a little desperate. College was coming and I was afraid 24/7. My SAT scores were, to put it mildly, awful. My vocational assessment was equally bad and suggested I was not suited to college. I was pretty sure my grade point average might get me into the door at an institution of higher learning and my SAT scores would send me right back out. Thinking there was not much hope, I applied to only one school, a strategy which makes absolutely no sense. Well, it does make a little sense. I mean, my sister was there at the university, a fact that gave me some comfort. I figured being with her at the U of W was way better than being alone somewhere else. She had her own life, so it wasn't as though I would be able to tag along with her as I had done so many times before, but I was clinging to anything familiar as I looked at what appeared to be the biggest mountain I had ever climbed.

BEAUTY FROM ASHES

Though I planned to graduate from high school without revealing my secrets related to learning disabilities, something inside me yearned to shout the truth from the rooftops. I felt misunderstood; I felt tired; I felt burned out. I was limping to the finish line but felt I didn't have much to show for it. Success as I had defined it, grades, and a cheer sweater were not fulfilling. I wished I could remember why I was running. Putting my story on paper to get credit in English had made me even surer I was missing something. I had been running toward a goal, but for what?

On a particularly rough day, when I felt like I couldn't push on, my mom said something profound. Her exact words were, "I hope someday you will use your story to help someone else. That will make everything worth it." Use my story? Hmmm. I didn't know exactly what she meant. I put the idea in the back of my mind and wondered how a girl like me could make a difference.

Around this time I decided to compete in a local pageant. While this may seem akin to becoming a gymnast when you are known for tripping up and down flights of stairs, the idea was not completely ridiculous. I will admit that when a pageant representative came to our school to hand out applications, I was an unlikely candidate. I could sing but seldom had performed in public. The swimsuit category was iffy as I was sporting 25 extra pounds. Did I mention I was terrified of public speaking? The only reason I took the application was I heard the representative say that as Miss Northshore there would be an opportunity for service in the community. I thought this might be what my mom was talking about but wasn't sure how I—as Miss So and So—was going to make a difference. Oh, and there were several thousand dollars in scholarships at stake. With limited assistance for my next step in school, I knew scholarship money could turn a crazy idea into a goal worth considering. Okay, let's be honest. I was also a driven girl looking for another form of validation, probably believing that a banner would make me somebody. There, I said it.

For some unknown reason, I won the local pageant. The only part of the evening that was meaningful to me was when I gave a 10-second speech. With my knees knocking and my voice wavering, I did the unthinkable. It was common at that time to say in your speech how you had been dreaming of becoming Miss America since you were a child, but I chose to tell everyone I had learning disabilities and that my goal was to be an advocate for individuals experiencing special needs.

I didn't go on to win Miss Washington, I'm afraid. I knew immediately I was in over my head, competing against people far more seasoned than I. I would like to say that I brushed off the loss, but for someone as driven as I was, that was hard to do. Once again, though, God redeemed the situation and taught me I could make a difference without a banner.

Though typically Miss Northshore would attend ribbon-cutting ceremonies at hardware stores or wave from a passing car in a parade, I requested the opportunity to do community service in local schools. I didn't really have to do anything to get the ball rolling. One local newspaper article about a dyslexic queen who was graduating from high school with honors caused the phone to ring. With so many kids fighting the same battle against learning disabilities that I had, parents and teachers clung to my story and asked me to offer encouragement to their kids.

The very thing—public speaking—that had caused me to sweat in ninth grade was never an intentional move. If someone had said to me, "I want you to be a public speaker," I would have replied, "Not in a million years." The good news is it happened gradually; I sort of fell into it. I went from giving a 10-second speech in a pageant to speaking in a resource room at a nearby high school. I was terribly nervous, even about a speech that would be just a few sentences long. When it was over, I vowed to never do it again. Soon after I made this vow I got a call from a special education teacher requesting that I share my story with her students. I told my mom I didn't want to go.

Her response was, "When you were growing up, it would have been so great to know that someone else had gotten through and how they did it. You can do whatever you want, but you could make a difference for those kids." So there I would be again, doing the very thing that made me so scared.

I probably thought I was doing this "scary" thing to benefit someone else. The truth is, every time I spoke about my experiences, there was healing for me. All the grief from years of being called names and all the failure had a purpose. I still had a lot of work to do on myself, but this was the first step toward something positive.

With speaking opportunities and service work making demands on my time, I pulled further and further away from school. I attended class, but it was no secret I was done. My motivation for "leaving early" was all about self-preservation. I just couldn't fake who I was anymore. I found myself in a room of young strangers at a local elementary school being more honest than with any of the kids I had gone to school with for five years. Feeling it was too late to tell the truth, and not knowing how it would be received anyway, I just chose to pull away.

At our senior assembly my name in the program had a list of awards after it. I was fourth in my class with a 3.98 grade point average, a long-standing member of the honor society, and the recipient of a number of significant scholarships. I was so detached from my school experience at this point that even these accomplishments seemed trivial.

The last award given that morning, the ASB (Associated Student Body) Award, was voted on by students and given to an outstanding senior. When my name was called, I thought there had been a mistake (my usual response). I couldn't believe it, but there was the plaque with my name inscribed on it.

Holding the award in my hand made me realize I had come full circle. The little girl who wanted so much to fit in got her wish. Like so many goals reached or accomplishments achieved, though, there was still an overriding emptiness in me.

The deep-seated feeling that whatever bad things had happened in our lives was in some way my fault immersed me in low self-esteem, and I couldn't seem to rise above it. I held unrealistic views of my responsibility for other people's decisions and their happiness, and therefore, I couldn't ever feel joy or experience accomplishments. When holding a plaque that said essentially, "You are accepted and you have accomplished much," I still didn't feel that I was enough. It was never as clear as on that day that I needed to change the direction of my life. I wasn't sure how I was going to do it, but I committed to finding a new way to live.

13

College Sounds
Easier than It Is

College, graduate school, becoming a teacher and speaker—things no one would have believed possible when I sat in special education class as the leader of the misfits—would soon become realities. Finding healing and balance in my personal life and using my experiences for good as a speaker proved to be terribly difficult for the likes of me. With God's help I learned that even someone who writes backward and often gets lost can make a difference.

Entering college should have been the realization of a dream. This was what my mom had asked me to do so many years ago, but though I was taking the right step, I was terribly conflicted. I mean, I had gotten through high school, but that was a much smaller environment. After being accepted to the University of Washington, I wondered how I was going to find my way around a campus measured in miles with a population of students numbering 60,000. I also feared what would happen to my mom when I left. Having viewed myself as her caretaker, I used her addiction and ongoing friction with my dad as a reason not to move on. It was a convenient excuse for nearly missing an opportunity.

With home life issues as a backdrop, I entered college already on shaky ground. The minute I walked away from our house I was paralyzed with fear. Even dysfunction had its comfort. Now there was little that was familiar, and it felt like my feet were not touching the ground. Soon academic stresses would compound the situation and leave me completely disoriented.

As if a curtain dropped and rose again, I suddenly found myself in my sister's sorority house—as pledge class president, no less. I remember going through "rush" and pledging a house, but it was as if these decisions were made in a fog. If I had been using my head, I would have lived at home (even with the issues there) and gone to a community college, taking small steps away from high school. Instead, I made one big leap. Thankfully, following in my sister's footsteps led me to a safe living environment, but I was so far out of my element that I felt like I was making decisions without enough perspective and consideration.

On the first day of school I knew I was in trouble. After walking a mile, I arrived at my first class out of breath and sweating. Late, I found that my classroom was actually an auditorium filled with hundreds of students. Those hoping to wait-list the class sat on the stairs and overflowed into the hall. With no seats available I leaned against the wall and tried to take notes.

The brochures for the University of Washington didn't indicate my classes would be so big that I wouldn't be able to see (and in my case hear) my professors. Nor did they mention that when you needed help from a professor, you would only have the opportunity to get it during a half-hour session offered every other Tuesday at 4 P.M. This was to accommodate all 900 students in my Psychology 101 class, by the way. The professors never had to worry about me coming to their office hours; I seldom could find their locations in obscure buildings on the huge campus.

Did I mention the reading and writing required at this level was so significant I was behind on the first day? The smell of failure was in the air.

While learning disabilities shouldn't prevent you from going to college, it is a difficult road. You need to minimize your schedule and stay focused. Changes in housing, peer groups, culture, and academic demands can make even the best student feel overwhelmed. I would have needed to simplify my schedule on a much greater level if I was going to succeed.

In my effort to fit in, I participated in the same activities as everyone else. I stayed up late attending "exchanges" (events with other houses and fraternities), then struggled to rise at 4 A.M. to study until breakfast. After attending class all day, I would study for as many hours as possible, but my efforts were thwarted by countless distractions.

When you are new to the house you have to study with your pledge class. Though the environment was kept quiet, I would look around the room randomly and get off task easily. Without a filter system, a room filled with people studying where the light was too bright was just never going to work for me. I heard and saw everything, and it made me feel totally disrupted. Longing for pure silence I found my refuge in a storage closet located in our laundry room. I spent the early hours of morning holed up in the closet until someone ran the first load of laundry. Sometimes I was able to get in three hours of studying before I was interrupted.

Finding a quiet place to study was only one of the challenges I faced. Though I had developed some good study skills over the years, nothing worked very well in my new environment. I would study more, using all of my techniques, and still not comprehend and retain the college-level information. Every time I would fail a quiz, I told myself I just needed to study more. I kept adding more time to my regimen until there were no longer any more hours in the day.

One of the most significant problems I had in terms of college-level academics was my writing. Don't get me wrong. I was having a really difficult time keeping up with my reading assignments too, but that was a behind-the-scenes issue only revealed by my test scores. My writing, on the other hand, was giving me away on a daily basis. I was definitely turning in work below the standard expected from an incoming freshman.

Writing issues affected my note taking, essay tests, written assignments, and correspondence with professors and teacher assistants. If I had had access to a computer, things might have been better. Technology as we know it today, with laptops and personal computers, was nonexistent. There might have been one person in our whole house who had a word processor, which was a glorified typewriter. Typewriters, not word processors, were the most common assistive devices, and my skill at the keyboard was less than stellar. I used so much Wite-Out when typing, I actually broke my typewriter by disfiguring keys that hit the thick liquid too many times.

Even when I hired someone to type my work, there were problems. With my final drafts laden with mistakes and my handwriting hard to decipher, it was difficult for the typist to create a product worthy of turning in.

I did well in what were called "quiz sections" where you verbally discuss the material from a week's worth of classes. The teacher assistants running the discussion groups would have spoken positively about my grasp of the content and my overall participation. The problem is none of my understanding displayed in quiz sections was transferred to tests and quizzes. When grades were listed from highest to lowest on long sheets of computer paper posted on the lecture hall wall, my name was often at the bottom. Long hours of study had not been effective.

I would like to blame all these problems on the type of tests that were given. The truth is, I do not do well with Scantron test forms. Lowercase B and D look just alike to me, especially under pressure. When pressed for time, I find my dyslexia seems to get worse, I don't track well, and I end up filling in the wrong circles. I seldom can see the problem when I am reviewing, so the test is turned in with many incorrect answers. I would love to say that when I failed an essay test it was the blue test booklet's fault, but that is just not a believable excuse. My writing in the blue test booklet was actually the problem. Whether Scantron or blue book, I seemed to fail or semi-fail at whatever test I touched.

I knew deep in my heart my abilities were in question. Just as when I found myself in honors classes in eighth grade, I often asked myself, "How did I get here?" The feeling that any moment I would be found to be incompetent kept me in a heightened state of anxiety. Already stressed with the basics of getting my schoolwork done, I found test days unbearable; my body would actually tremble I was so nervous. On more than one occasion I was so overcome with fear I actually sat down in the wrong room and began to take a test for the wrong class.

By the end of my first quarter in school I had a nearly failing grade in two of my three classes, resulting in my lowest grade point average in six years. Knowing I was establishing a GPA in college, I had purposefully taken three classes, and the credit load was only 12 instead of 15. Already behind in credits and realizing by anyone's standards I was not doing well, I considered alternatives. Drop out, go to another school, or regroup and find help.

On the day I got my first college report card, I started calling directory assistance of the University of Washington and asking if there were any services available for learning-disabled students. I was not very specific. It was like standing in the middle of Red Square (a main intersection among four enormous buildings in the center of the campus) and yelling, "Help!" I don't know why I thought the operators should know how to direct my call, but I felt frustrated when every call I made over the course of the next two quarters led me straight to a dead end.

Even though my grades looked a little sketchy and my collegiate status looked tentative, my personal life was about to take a positive turn.

A White Knight Driving a Company Car

One day, after a particularly negative conversation with a "significant other," I took a long, hard look at myself. I had been going to counseling for some time and the effect was profoundly positive. I came away from talks with my counselor feeling less responsible for everything. I also was feeling less and less tied to the idea that a high grade point average made me somebody. Good timing considering my most recent report card. The problem of determining my value based on superficial means was still there, though. I was still clinging to the old ideas—focusing on whether someone liked me, not whether I liked myself.

Crippling self-esteem issues led me to keep peers at a distance and be hyper aware of the possibility of judgment. Those same self-esteem issues had the opposite effect on my relationships with boys/men. I did not think critically about relationships. If anyone gave me a second look, I felt lucky. I concentrated on being liked, not being accepted for who I was. It was all about "Do they like me?" not "Should I like them?" The handwriting was on the wall for me if I didn't turn things around. I was going to be eternally miserable and probably divorced by 30 if I didn't make some better choices.

For not being a very good decision maker in terms of relationships, I was about to make one good decision. I called my boyfriend and let him know the relationship was over. I promptly walked into my room, got a sheet of notebook paper, and wrote a list. The list started with the words, "Dear God, please enable me to make better choices in relationships. I pray for this man to come into my life." I then wrote over 30 qualities and character traits I prayed this man would have. I folded the list and put it in my Bible. I stopped dating altogether and committed myself to God's will.

My list was created in October. By the end of January, I met him. Turns out the "list man" was a Midwestern guy transplanted to Seattle with his first job out of college. He came to a rehearsal for a charity production I was involved with and that was the end of our search. Turns out he too had a list.

After meeting Dave I decided to stay at the University of Washington but moved home to lower the distraction level in my life. I was sure I would do better in school if I didn't have to compete with the noise and activities of the sorority house. Moving home was just geography. All I did was exchange new distractions for old ones. My grades still didn't improve.

While deeply frustrated with school, I continued to make calls to directory assistance at the university. All of them led me nowhere. One cheerful operator (I'm kidding about the cheerful part) heard the frustration in my voice and suggested I contact the office of mental health services. I kept my comments to myself but hoped this individual was joking. Though at this point my mental health *was* in question, I continued to hold out hope that "talk" therapy was not my only option.

I have heard it said that successful people are not necessarily smarter than others, they just never give up. I don't know if this is true, but I'd like to think it is. Either stubborn or stupid, I was not willing to give up on college. After countless tries, I called the University of Washington directory assistance one more time. I told the operator what I was looking for, and she said, "I will connect you." I was wondering if someone was about to offer me three free counseling sessions.

Well, it turns out there is a place called the Disabled Student Service (DSS) at the University of Washington. Operators must have known this office existed, but I was not asking for it specifically by name. This conundrum nearly cost me a chance at college.

After meeting with the director of DSS I learned current tests documenting my learning disabilities would enable me to receive a variety of services. Hmmm. Current tests. I didn't have any tests. Now what? I was told that I could be retested, and then I would be eligible for services.

Eight hours at the Washington Association for Children and Adults with Learning Disabilities later, I was officially learning disabled. The tests revealed I have a below-average IQ and learning disabilities so severe I shouldn't do very well in college. While this was not exactly a compliment, I had heard worse from kids on the playground in elementary school.

I wasn't heartbroken over some of the things said in the commentary section of my tests. It was suggested I should be doing even worse than I currently was, so I held on to that and tried to be proud I had limped along.

With my tests on file, I immediately became a part of the DSS and received many services, including:

- Longer testing times
- Testing in a quiet room with a proctor
- Audio books
- Front-row seating
- Natural lighting in testing rooms
- Tutors
- Lecture notes
- Alternative forms of evaluation
- Tape recorders

Letters outlining my special needs were sent in advance of all my classes to ensure that professors and their assistants were aware and could plan for my needs.

I not only received support from the people who directed the DSS, I networked with other students experiencing similar academic challenges. Though coordinating and communicating my needs with the DSS took extra time, it was well worth the effort.

Over time I took the advice of academic counselors at DSS and tried new strategies and assistive devices. It was not long before my book bag was overflowing with tape recorders, earphones, tapes, batteries, books, audio books, flash cards, highlighters, lecture notes from the U of W note-taking service, my own lecture notes, and copies (carbon or photo copied) of lecture notes from fellow students. Where were backpacks on wheels when you needed them?

Though my book bag was heavy, I had a renewed sense of

enthusiasm about school. I still chose to take fewer credits, but did much better in my classes due to the services offered by DSS.

It is important to mention that in conjunction with my testing for learning disabilities, I also pursued long-overdue testing for food allergies at a specialty clinic called Hope. Having done scratch tests and blood tests through our family doctor, I knew I had allergies to environmental agents. What couldn't be explained was why I was sick all the time. Along with respiratory ailments such as bronchitis and ear infections, I developed migraines causing temporary bouts of blindness in both eyes due to "auras" and painful stomachaches.

After extensive testing I learned I am pretty much allergic to all food. Well, not all food—just everything that tastes good. I decided to remove everything I was allergic to from my diet. Foods I omitted included:

- Milk and all milk-related products, including derivatives of milk such as casein and sodium casinate
- All forms of flour, except brown rice
- All forms of soy and soy-based products, including soybean oil
- Tomatoes, avocados, and onions
- Eggs
- Bananas
- Spices
- All nuts
- All citrus fruits
- Chocolate

• Corn and corn-related products
• All forms of oil except olive oil
• All packaged, processed, and cured food and meat
• All foods containing preservatives
• All products containing any form of gluten.

My exciting diet was rice based and everything had to be made from scratch. I immediately lost 35 pounds. A great result from a drastic dietary change for sure, but every day I longed for peanut butter and wished for even one chocolate chip.

Though my allergies have improved to a certain degree thanks to alternative treatments, I still have many limitations. While substitutes for certain foods are more plentiful, they are also expensive. You can break the bank buying one box of wheat-free cookies. Due to the prohibitive cost of ready-made products, I have opted to make some of my own recipes. My husband and children will tell you that "my food"—including wheat-free, gluten-free, dairy-free, and soy-free creations—is often taste-free too! Let's just put it this way: No one ever fights me for my cashew butter cookies. Though I pretend my food tastes good, I will admit my rice-crust pizza does taste like wallpaper. I have no personal experience with eating wallpaper, but I'm making an educated guess. Even with exciting developments in using rice, tapioca, and garbanzo bean flour, I often catch myself looking longingly at someone eating "real" chocolate cake and have to remind myself not to drool.

With few options in terms of what I could eat, moving home became an even more necessary decision. In addition to having more control over my diet, I had more time to study in a quieter environment. My mom and I did the dance of "who is taking care of whom," but with Dave's help and a strong commitment to a church, I was better able to create boundaries.

Marriage and Other Things that Scared Me

After two years of dating, Dave asked me to marry him. I said, "Yes." After saying yes, I hoped he might forget the whole idea if I let enough time pass. Nothing against Dave, but I didn't exactly hold a high opinion of the institution of marriage. I was a girl who still kept her belongings in boxes just in case things didn't work out. Thank goodness Dave had patience. While I worried (big surprise), God worked on my heart enabling me to see that divorce, remarriage, and broken families were a part of my past but did not have to be replicated in my future. Dave and I were married on June 18, 1988.

The Most Unlikely Public Speaker in the World

I am going to repeat myself here, but I am the least likely person to give a speech—to anyone, anywhere! I used to stutter and I can't read under pressure and, and, and . . . How in the world did I go from volunteering in resource rooms in my hometown to speaking to thousands of educators, parents, and students at a time? You could say it was luck, but I think Someone may have been involved (point finger up at this point). No, I don't think my mom paid anyone off, but she did attend many a speech in banquet rooms where she prayed no one would drop a dish—a surefire way to make me forget my whole speech. Even with an inconsistent brain, somehow I was invited all over the country to share my story.

As thrilling as it was to be invited to speak, I had the worst time getting my nerves under control. While I may have looked composed, under my pastel suit I was a big coward. I didn't just have a hard time delivering the speech, I worried before the speech, worried during the speech, and then contemplated my effectiveness after the speech. If I had a speech in two weeks, there was probably not a minute out of the two weeks I didn't worry about the speech. I am still reminded of the day (not because I want to remember, but because Dave won't let me forget it) Dave asked me to go to a movie. I said I couldn't because I had a speech. He said, "But your speech isn't until tonight. We have plenty of time if we go to a matinee."

I said, "No, I need to spend the afternoon worrying."

You probably think I was kidding when I said that. I wasn't.

I was traveling all over the United States and Canada speaking to wide and varied audiences. I am a person who gets numbers and letters backward and can't find her way around a mall, but there I was in unfamiliar cities trying to navigate airports, ground transportation, and lodging. The one positive aspect is that being preoccupied with getting lost gave me less time to worry about speaking.

I quickly learned to protect myself by having my host provide transportation on-site and relied on airport personnel to make sure I found the right gates. While nerve-wracking, it was also freeing to know that even with limitations, I could find my way.

The most interesting of all the audiences I ever spoke to were those made up of prisoners. Inspired by a newspaper article about the number of incarcerated people afflicted with learning disabilities, I inquired about opportunities to serve as a volunteer in our prison system. Dave would accompany me with his trusty guitar in hand. Together we provided concerts for inmates before I shared my story.

The number of "hardened criminals" I saw cry because they identified with my story eventually numbered in the thousands. Grown men and women shed tears because they too had been called names and were underestimated due to mild to severe learning disabilities. While not an excuse for criminal activity, it was easy to see how someone who doesn't think it is possible to learn can be lost to another side of life.

While keeping up a steady schedule of speaking, I chipped away at my degree. I intended to get a bachelor of arts degree in psychology but wasn't sure I wanted to become a counselor. Though I was pretty sure I could offer better advice than I did the time I convinced a child afraid of a bully to walk home with me, I felt my heart moving in a different professional direction.

From the time I was little, I had always wanted to be a teacher but had given up on the idea because I thought it would never be possible due to my severe learning disabilities. Who would hire a teacher who writes backwards? That isn't exactly in line with professional standards for educators. Finding my way to speaking engagements through a fog of learning issues must have renewed my sense that anything was possible. I decided to explore the idea of teaching again.

Even with the help of the Disabled Student Services, my grades were not high enough to get into a fifth-year graduate program to obtain my teaching certification. An academic counselor suggested I take science and math classes at a local community college. With smaller classes and more access to assistance, I saw the first improvement in my grades in years.

The good news is I graduated from college. The bad news is it took me seven years. I tell people that it took so long to get my degree because I had to pay for all of it, but the full story is that a below-average IQ kind of slowed me down.

However long it took, I knew my BA in psychology would not mark the end of my studies. The trick was to not tell myself. Just like when I used to fib to myself by suggesting I only had to do the easiest assignment out of a daunting stack of homework, I knew it was always better to keep my psyche in the dark.

Even as I filled out the paperwork for the teaching program, I told myself white lies about how I might not make it into the program, and even if I did, I could always drop out. Of course, I had no intention of dropping out, even if the going was really rough, but telling falsehoods kept my fear of failure at a minimum. The day before I graduated from college, I was accepted into the teaching program. I continued to lull my fears by telling myself I had plenty of options if this didn't work out. I am glad I never asked myself to name those options. The truth is, there weren't any other options. I was clearly not going to medical school.

During the large general education classes for my undergraduate degree I struggled and even failed sometimes. Interestingly, though, even before I received services from DSS, I seemed to do better when I took classes in my major. Many of the classes in psychology were smaller, and I had more access to professors. In this atmosphere I often would do better. The same thing happened in the graduate teaching program. I used few if any services from DSS because the classes were smaller and I could get ongoing help from professors and TAs. It also helped that I really connected with the material being presented. Even if I was struggling, the material was so interesting I found it easier to stay engaged.

After a grueling year of in-class work, I entered the final phase of my teaching certification requirements. I became a student teacher in a fourth-grade classroom at an elementary school near my home. While totally filled with enthusiasm about this new endeavor, I encountered bumps along the way and was thankful I had students willing to put up with me while I learned.

It became clear that good teaching requires a tremendous amount of passion, commitment, and technique. I had the passion and commitment. The technique, well, that was born over time. With the help of a good master teacher, I was able to create lessons that worked, and I felt good about what I brought to my students. I was reminded again and again of what my teachers had done for me. Seeking to honor the gifts they had given inspired me even on days I felt like a failure. While I was humbled again and again during my student teaching, I never doubted my career choice.

After receiving my teaching certification, I substituted for a year and a half. I spent most of my time in junior high schools (because I was the only one who would go back). I did not apply for a full-time job because I had this crazy idea that I wanted to enter a master's degree program. Though my husband was exhausted from proofing my papers and was probably hoping I would come to my senses, I was determined to continue.

I was very nervous about returning to school in a full-fledged graduate capacity but kept my fears at bay by suggesting to my subconscious that I would probably never get in. In my search for graduate programs in education I found a perfect fit at a University of Washington satellite campus located close to my home.

While I had a high grade point average and good recommendation that should have qualified me for the program, there was one hitch in the application process that nearly derailed my efforts. To be accepted into the program, you had to get a reasonable score on the Graduate Record Exam. I would like to tell you that after intense study I "aced" the test. I didn't. While I was newly pregnant and plagued with morning sickness when I took the exam, there was no good excuse for my low score except for, well, the obvious. I had used all of the typical study preparation materials to prepare for the exam, but it was a timed test, held in a room built as if to heighten the echo-chamber effect (you truly could hear every paper rustle), and it featured fluorescent lights. The test itself contained material that— because I was under pressure—might as well have been written in a foreign language. Even questions about material I knew appeared only vaguely familiar.

Somehow my grade point average must have held more weight than my GRE scores because I was accepted into the program despite my low score. I attended school part-time while substituting and became among the first graduates to complete a master's degree in education emphasizing "at risk" students and multicultural issues.

My thesis project focused on creating a school at a community organization called Special Delivery. Special Delivery provided housing and support services for women in a crisis situation due to unplanned pregnancy and parenting. Having started as a volunteer "advocate" (providing support and mentoring to a resident), I learned that education was emphasized in the mission statement for Special Delivery, but no plan existed to implement any academic programs.

My master's program encouraged students to find needs within the community and fill them. Therefore, I felt led to create a school held at Special Delivery. Open to the community and attended by all the residents that required housing, it would be the perfect blend of teaching and service.

My students came to class with some very interesting histories. One enthusiastic student exclaimed on our first night of class that she had first met me in jail. I nodded in agreement, but had to delicately clarify for my class that I was in jail as a volunteer speaker. My student may have been incarcerated due to drug offenses, but she felt a kinship with me because we had met before. It was a good start to an otherwise rocky relationship.

Women ages 13 to 33 came to my program needing remedial help, GED preparation, college-prep assistance, and other social, emotional, and educational support. Given the daunting task of teaching resistant and, in some cases, learning-disabled students, I enlisted the help of another volunteer. A teacher and librarian at a neighboring public elementary school, Mary helped me start, refine, and maintain the Educational Services Program at Special Delivery.

Some of my students just needed a little boost, while others had dropped out of school as early as eighth grade. Early parenting, addiction, home life issues, and/or diagnosed and undiagnosed learning issues preempted their time or progress in school, causing every one of my students to be resistant to some aspect of education. My job was to help them overcome fear, give them the tools to get up to grade level, and become prepared for the next step academically.

I didn't always see the fruit of my labor upon their departure from Special Delivery, but often after time and reflection my students went on to do some great things. On many occasions I received phone calls from young women who graduated from my class and went on to college or some other form of training.

When I graduated from my master's degree program, I actually felt the accomplishment fully. My sister was the first in our family on both sides to go to college. I was the first to go to graduate school. I accepted my diploma, and my life felt complete. In the audience were my family, my husband, and my son. It was a very proud moment.

Two years after graduating with my master's degree, I was enjoying my work at Special Delivery and had seen significant growth in the program, but when I learned that I was pregnant with our second child, I knew that it was time to go. I was determined to finish an endorsement in special education before our baby arrived and knew that I couldn't do that and work at Special Delivery too. I resigned my position and went back to school.

Just after Jessica was born, I finished my endorsement in special education. While my certification enabled me to teach general education K-8, my endorsement allowed me to teach special education K-12.

With two children under the age of five, I was not quite ready to take on a full-time position as a teacher. I managed to find a full-time position related to education anyway—or should I say I created one? Having been a speaker for quite a number of years, I had seen the power of a real-life story to inspire people. That prompted me to teach young people how to share the lessons they had learned by combining their life stories with music and dance to create an assembly program that looked like a concert with a message.

Many years later Positive Programs Inc. has provided inspirational assembly programs and after-school leadership classes to tens of thousands of students in the Northwest. Thanks to a non-profit license and experienced grant writers, we have stayed afloat financially and provided training and jobs for countless young people from "at risk" backgrounds. It has inspired many kids to act with courage, character, and commitment, even in difficult times.

I am always keenly aware of where I came from and how fortunate I am to have had positive leaders in my life. My deep desire to honor all the wonderful people who helped me will continue to fuel my work in the field of education for many years to come.

BRIDGES OVER TROUBLED WATERS

Just when I had things pretty well balanced—two parents, two kids, speaking, and teaching—life took an interesting turn. That interesting turn was a set of twins named Kelly and Chloe. We were the people who weren't supposed to be able to have children. We now have four. Let that be a lesson to you. A fertility drug and God's grace brought us Michael, an insulin drug and God's grace brought us Jessica. We stopped trying, and by God's grace had twins. Once again, let that be a lesson to you. When people tell me having children later in life has its benefits, I know what they are going to say: "You have more wisdom and patience." All I can say is, I would trade wisdom and patience for quickness and speed any day (and I'm hyperactive, remember).

Having children, being married, and growing in my faith has allowed me to gain perspective about my past and realize what is important. Gaining perspective allowed me to love my parents for who they are and view my childhood and any painful experiences I went through as part of the journey. I've learned to trust that God can redeem even the most difficult circumstances and make them something you can learn from.

Even though there had been so much healing over the years in my life, and even within my family, there were still some mountains to climb.

While sitting at an Easter dinner at my sister's house a few years ago, my son, Michael, asked, "Why isn't grandpa here? Why doesn't he ever celebrate Easter or Christmas with us?"

My sister and I looked at each other and were speechless. We had been celebrating separate holidays with our parents for so long that we no longer knew why. Well, the reason was tension between my parents, but the question from my son made it clear that nothing should prevent our family from being together. While there was a little resistance at first, my sister declared we would be celebrating every holiday together from that time forward. And we all lived happily ever after . . . um . . . sort of. A few bumps along the way later, everyone learned to work together. and it has been great to have everyone under the same roof a few times a year.

Family relationships can be an adventure, right? I used to think that one day you could actually reach perfection within your family. Everyone would get along, and it would all be idyllic. What? I am not sure where I got that idea, but I am fully recovered from my faulty thinking now. Nothing is ever perfect, but we can do the best with what we have and try to be graceful even in difficult circumstances. While I don't know how to make everything perfect, I do know I love all of the members of my family.

While we will always seek to do better, there is lots to be proud of. With eight children between my sister and me (grandchildren for my parents), there are sixteen eyes and ears watching, listening, and learning. The good news is that the children have seen our family move toward reconciliation. I am forever grateful God saw fit to allow us the opportunity to experience healing in our lifetime. This relational healing within our family, along with my mom's sobriety since 1985, provides a powerful legacy that has been passed on to the next generation.

The title of this book was inspired by a wonderful poem titled "A Bag of Tools," written by Robert L. Sharpe in 1890:

Isn't it strange that princes and kings,
And clowns that caper in sawdust rings,
And common people like you and me
Are builders for eternity?

Each is given a bag of tools,
A shapeless mass, a book of rules;
And each must make, ere life is flown
A stumbling block, or a steppingstone.

I believe, just as the poem suggests, that we are all given gifts, opportunities, and even challenges. Every day we have the chance to decide what we are going to do with what we are given—rise above or stay where we are. As much as I believe we have a choice in how we will respond to what we have been given, especially when we are young or when the challenges we face are significant, it is no longer about whether we will rise above, but whether we can. In my case I can honestly say that without the help of teachers, family members, and other supportive people, I am not sure what would have become of me.

For as long as I live I will be grateful that the little girl I used to be was given a chance. It would have been so easy to lower expectations and never ask me to try. In the end no one could have faulted such logic. Previous performance or lack of it was all anyone would have needed to justify low expectations.

The disabilities and handicapping conditions I have been diagnosed with should have prevented me from having a full life. Thankfully, that isn't where the story ended. Because I was encouraged to try, and shown other ways to succeed when conventional methods didn't work, I found hope and eventually success in areas of academics no one would have thought possible.

I owe a great deal of thanks to every mentor who ever said in so many ways, "You can do it!" Because of their support, I have reached goals beyond my wildest dreams and will continue their mission in hopes others will be inspired to reach their goals, for it is then that my stumbling blocks will truly become stepping stones.

14 ✏

Suggestions
for Parents
and Educators

*H*aving been a child diagnosed with learning disabilities, a teacher of learning-disabled and at-risk students, as well as a mother of a child born with a cleft lip and cleft palate, I have personally seen various perspectives of families of special-needs children. Though I would have never hoped to be on the "other side of the conference table" receiving an IEP (individualized education plan) written about one of my children, it is just one in a long line of humbling experiences that remind me where I came from. By tangling with insurance companies over a procedure for my son and begging our school district for necessary services, I learned to be polite but persistent.

After going through major reconstructive surgery at age 10 weeks, chronic ear infections and hearing loss, permanent tubes, and a never-ending series of respiratory ailments, our son, Michael, stood as a monument to the resiliency of children. Unable to blow out a candle or whistle as a result of the structure of his palate, Michael was still the pied piper among children in our neighborhood. He was so even-tempered and warmhearted, I could hardly wait for the rest of the world to meet him.

When Michael had just turned five, we had no qualms about his entering kindergarten. As he was our first child, we had no comparisons to make. All we knew was that Michael was brilliant. He entered our neighborhood public school, and we waited to get the call about the need to pass him to the next grade or the notice about entry to the gifted program.

Instead of word about the gifted program, I received calls from his teacher who seemed to be at her wit's end. Apparently Michael was . . . busy. Gee, where do you think he got that? While not alarmed (I knew busy wasn't fatal), I sensed the teacher felt "busy" meant bad. I tried to quell her concerns by getting involved in the classroom. Being on-site meant I soon was seeing the "problem" and it wasn't Michael. Yes, it is true: Michael liked to move. To deal with his energy he would wiggle in his seat and raise his hand a lot.

Instead of seeing Michael's energy as a gift, he was viewed as a behavior problem. To be honest, I wonder how the scar on his lip played into this whole thing because there were other kids with the same "busyness." I noticed that if three kids were running, only one would be stopped by the teacher and reprimanded. Guess who? On more than one occasion she justified her response by saying Michael was running faster.

The longer I tried to put a shine on the situation, the worse things got. Finally, I was told to have Michael tested. The word *medication* came up. I saw where this was all leading. I was being asked to medicate a five-year-old because he was nice but irritating. Last time I checked, "nice but irritating" wasn't a formal diagnosis.

Wait. Before I go on with this story, I want to clarify one thing, because I know what some of you are thinking. *She's one of those people—against medication for children with ADHD and other behavior-related issues. Or maybe she's one of those people who thinks medication is fine for other people, but not for her kid. Or maybe she just thinks that if kids ate more whole grains and watched less TV, ADHD wouldn't exist.* Nope! Um, I was the poster child for ADHD. I know it is a real physical issue. When I was very small, anyone who spent more than five minutes with me told my mom about a medication called Ritalin. She thought it was considered experimental at the time, though. Unsure about such an approach, she chose not to use medication. I learned to run around my head and order my world to cope, but I'm glad I found something that worked for me. In the end we will never know if I would have benefited from medication. (Well, I think we all know I would have!) While I didn't have the assistance of medication, at least my sock drawer was tidy. Did I mention that I made lines on our carpet?

I do believe that some kids learn by moving. Busyness is part of their nature, and to squelch this desire to move while thinking might cause them to lose interest in academics altogether or think they aren't smart, because they aren't allowed to learn in an area of their strength. Other kids will settle down if given time to mature and some strategies to cope positively with their energy. Still other kids will find that any learning experiences—even social experiences—are frustrating without the assistance of medication.

Thankfully, we now have more experience with ADHD and related issues. We know medication is the appropriate measure in some cases, but parents always have the right to look for other options. The most important thing we can do is prevent misdiagnosis by ensuring that we look critically at the physical health, social and emotional development, and academic progress of each child and consult with specialists so we can make informed choices. We now know that medication, if administered without educational and behavior counseling, will not ensure greater success in the long term. We need to determine if ADHD really is the problem and if so, be sure to include behavior and educational strategies and counseling as a part of the overall treatment plan.

(Whew! Now I can go on with this story.)

By November the kid who went to school smiling lost the gleam in his eye. The more his teacher reprimanded him for being, well, a boy, the less he liked going to school.

Trying to make the situation work, but unwilling to medicate, I campaigned for Michael. I thought everyone would agree with me that given one more year (returning him to pre-K), Michael would likely settle down and be fine. If not, then we could pursue testing and diagnosis. After I talked with the teacher, school nurse, vice principal, principal, secretary, and anyone else who would listen, the response was clear. Medicate your child. Furthermore, I was told if I followed through with

my plan to move him back to pre-K, I would cause him psychological harm and his peers would shun him.

Knowing we were in charge (after all, we were the parents),
I stopped campaigning, I stopped talking, and I started doing.
I knew Michael needed more time. It was my fault this brilliant
kid was being labeled a problem. He was a big-motor boy in a
seat-oriented classroom. Shame on me for not having figured
this out. He should have been in pre-K in the first place, but
I didn't want to hold him back when I knew he was so smart.
Sometimes though, the way things are taught and a child's readiness to learn are not in sync. My goof was not a tragedy but was
going to have to be unraveled. Against the administration and
teacher's directive we took him out of kindergarten and placed
him in a private pre-K program.

Michael thrived in his new environment and made friends
quickly. His academic progress was right on target and he was
happy again. The same school I moved him from allowed him
to continue speech therapy for the rest of the year, but neither
he nor I was treated very well. He was switched to a different
speech therapist who often seemed annoyed with Michael and
suggested he was distracted during speech sessions. Strange—this
comment was never made until I chose to leave the school.

The next year, when Michael did not return to his former
school, he was denied access to speech therapy even though his
IEP provided for it. I was told his speech problems were not as
bad as other kids' and that he would probably be fine. Huh? Once
again, I thought it strange these statements were not made until
I removed him from the school. When I went to the director of

special education to ask for help, she made arrangements for him to receive speech assistance but only during the part of the day when he was in kindergarten. That meant he would have missed important subjects. I suggested to the director of special education that we were being treated unfairly. I was told kids "at the school" had first priority in terms of scheduling and took precedence over a child coming to receive therapy from another school.

I could have fought. I wanted to fight, but I learned to pick my battles. By now I had a second child with chronic ear infections, and I decided the energy I was expending was not well placed. I found speech therapy elsewhere.

After we moved Michael out of his kindergarten class and into pre-K, I had to pray a lot to find forgiveness for the teacher and the situation we left behind. My husband had recently left mortgage finance (and a company car) to become an associate pastor (a direct career path, as I'm sure you can see). This was perfect timing financially to take on high tuition bills—a given since we had no intention of returning Michael to our local public school. Worry about tuition was compounded as we saw his teacher often at church. Every time I saw her, I would feel the sting of her words from those early phone calls and meetings about Michael. Everything she said about him at the time and regarding his future had been negative.

On occasion she stopped my husband and asked how Michael was doing. We weren't sure if she was hoping her predictions were right or wrong. Our feelings of anxiety about what had happened increased when another parent from Michael's former kindergarten class stopped us about a year after our departure and said with a deeply concerned expression, "How is Michael doing? Is he going to be okay?" The suggestion was that Michael was either mentally unsettled or chronically ill. We later learned some things had been said about him upon his exit to suggest that Michael was (roll your eyes here) "unstable."

Though I had put this situation to rest, I continued to pray about it. Every time I felt a pang of hurt, I would pray more. Three years after we had moved Michael out of her class, his former teacher apologized. Over time she had come to realize that in her effort (and I honestly believe she intended to do the right thing) to "help" Michael, she had forced us out of public education. Realizing the financial burden for us, she felt badly and wondered how things could have been different if she had handled the situation in another way. She felt her behavior had bordered on being unprofessional and offered her heartfelt apology. I give her a lot of credit for doing this.

God took a tough situation and gave us new direction. He further healed the situation by bringing an apology. The good news is we didn't expect it or wait for it. We just did what we needed to do for Michael.

I would like to tell you the private school I moved Michael to was perfect. It is important to note, nothing ever is. The next year his kindergarten teacher took one look at his scar and his "busyness" and placed him in a chair isolated from the rest of the students. A few days into the year I noticed his placement and inquired about it. I was told that while Michael was a very nice boy, he wiggled a lot. Hadn't I heard this before? When I politely told the teacher that it was not acceptable to separate

Michael (a boy who did not have behavior problems except for wiggling) she reported to me that he loved the "special chair."

I said, "If it is so special, then I am sure every child in the class will love the chair, and unless every child is going to be sitting in it for the same length of time and for the same reason (its specialness), I would kindly request you never place my child in the "special chair" again. We had a great relationship after that. Just kidding. She left the school at the end of the year and took her special chair with her. All in all she wasn't a horrible teacher, just a little tired. She didn't harm Michael, but I am pretty sure she didn't like me. I could have moved classrooms and made a big deal. In this case I just stayed tuned in and was there to advocate when the need arose. Somehow it all worked out.

How much time do you have? Because I have a lot of stories, and my guess is you do too. As we reflect on our experiences as parents, there might be enough time and distance to see the absurdity and even humor of what we have gone through to help our children. If you can't find the humor yet, maybe you can at least find closure. If you can't find closure, keep praying. It will come.

I share these stories in no way to disparage a specific teacher or school setting that has been a part of my children's education experience so far. I do so to demonstrate that even if you have a child who doesn't experience a specific learning disability, attention issue, or physical challenge, you can find yourself talking special education and medication because they are, well, fidgety. Kids are so different. They could thrive in one environment and wither in another based on the number of times they are allowed to get out of their seats or some other factor that wouldn't apply to you and me, but makes or breaks whether they learn or not. For those of us who do have children with special needs, the challenges associated with finding what works and helping our kids achieve success academically and beyond can be fraught with difficulties, but the same rules apply in all scenarios. Be flexible and tenacious in finding what works best for your child in terms of setting, style, and method.

You are your child's best advocate. Don't ever leave it to someone else to know what is best for your child. Don't ever leave it to a test to determine your child's future. Be willing to look for the "right answers" no matter what it takes. Sometimes the answers will come from trial and error, and that's okay. Just remain dogged in your pursuit of answers for your child, especially when the obvious isn't the right direction.

I would like to reassure you that your effort to help your child will be always met with enthusiasm and immediate assistance. Well . . . I can't. People are people and they are imperfect. Oh, and I should mention that we live in a fallen world. So that means the path to raising our children and getting them the help they need isn't going to be smooth. If you know that going in, you don't have to be cynical. You just need to expect and pray for the very best in people and institutions. When you don't get it, start yelling . . . I mean, pray for direction and be willing to call, write, ask, or research until you find the right answer, the right doctor, the right school, the right teacher, the right procedure, the right approach.

It would be easy to blame everyone else in a difficult situation; after all, that is the most satisfying thing to do, right? It is important in all things that we contemplate our own behavior first and make sure everything we do is a reflection of our morals and faith.

Sometimes you might need to cry a little. Maybe you're going to need to cry a lot. The journey might have already been long for you as a parent, but don't despair. Take a deep breath, say a prayer, and forge ahead. God gave you the gift of your child. Don't give up just because someone in authority says something negative about your child or his or her future.

What Should You Do When You Don't Know What to Do?

If it has been suggested to you or you suspect that your child might have some type of learning, behavior, or physical issue, be swift to act. That action could include testing, research, or looking into different forms of schooling. It might require changing teachers or schools, changing doctors, and/or finding the right specialist. Before you move forward, though, be sure you have all the necessary information. You don't want to change schools when all you need to do is change teachers, or medicate a child to calm a particular behavior when all you need to do is get your child involved in sports.

Before you begin your search for assistance, ask yourself some questions:

- What should I do first?
- What can I do to prevent wasted time and/or a misdiagnosis?
- Who should I ask questions of?
- Who should I listen to?

- Am I ready to listen?
- Am I ready to act?
- Do I have all of the background information I need to begin my search?
- Have I ruled out issues that could mask the real problem?
- Am I making quick decisions out of fear, or am I moving swiftly, armed with background information about my child and the possible issue affecting him or her?
- Do I know about special education law and how it affects my child?
- When a particular setting or method isn't working for my child, how can I be diplomatic yet still advocate for my child?
- What does my child need to know so he or she can advocate for himself or herself but be protected from unnecessary or hurtful information?
- What battles are worth the time and energy? How do I make that distinction?
- How can I vent about a situation but do so without hurting anyone—especially my child?
- Where do I begin?

What Should I Do First?

I grew up watching people make decisions out of fear. My mom married quickly after my dad left to try to gain security. You learned how that turned out. Three cheers for quick decisions. When you make a swift move because you are trying to "right" something, you will almost always go in the wrong direction.

The lesson I learned from this type of decision making is that contrary to *Mulan* and every other Disney princess movie, following your heart won't always lead you to make the right decision. Our hearts are driven by emotions. Emotions are volatile and often send us careening off cliffs. Rather than acting reactively, take a moment (or several moments) and wait. Being still is hard for me because I am hyperactive to the highest degree. Because I am wired to move, I often want to jump in and fix a situation quickly. I have been called up short many times for being unfaithful in search of a quick remedy. Prayerful consideration will never be the wrong move.

Ask, Listen, then Act

As you begin to help your child, it's important to ask the right questions of the right people, listen intently, and be ready to act.

Notorious for not trusting myself when faced with a challenge for which I do not have an answer, I often begin asking everyone and his brother what I should do. I usually get a lot of opinions, a little good advice, and a recipe for a casserole. In the end my jaw is tired from talking, my ears are weak from listening, and all I have to show from the gab fest is more confusion. My suggestion is to trust the direction you have been given by faith, ask only those you trust and respect, then listen intently while preparing yourself to act.

I recently got a call from the aunt of a boy experiencing what is called a "spectrum disorder." Spectrum disorders have to do with sensory processing and are on the continuum with related disorders such as autism and Asperger's syndrome. The aunt had been referred to me for advice by someone who had heard me speak. I was more than willing to take her long-distance call and was happy to offer suggestions.

She relayed her story in full and with great detail. From her perspective, special education had failed this boy, and teachers and doctors were unsure what to do. Some "experts" had not even heard the term "spectrum disorder" before, she said, sounding exasperated. As the aunt, she was simply calling me to gather information she thought would be helpful to her sister. What I knew almost before I opened my mouth to speak is that the woman on the other end of the line didn't want to listen.

I understand why people do this—ask, but not listen. When faced with challenges it's easy to get stuck or become overwhelmed. Like tires in mud we keep spinning our wheels, but don't go anywhere. Hurriedly, we gather information from every direction, then find ourselves too overloaded to respond to it. In this exhausted state we can feel every idea is too difficult or will take too long to give results or is too radical to consider.

Fear of making the wrong decision often keeps us from making any decision at all. This is another "tire in the mud" scenario that wastes precious time. The sooner we address a problem related to learning and development, the better the chance a child can recover, overcome, and/or compensate. When we shuffle our feet, we are losing precious moments that could be used to help our child.

Here is a tip. Don't spin your wheels by asking just anyone. When you do ask someone worthy of trust, check your heart and mind to see if you are ready to listen and if what they are saying seems sound in light of your faith and existing knowledge base. Then compare the advice you have been given to advice from another knowledgeable person in the field (second opinion) and move forward.

Do First Things First!

During the conversation with the aunt of the boy with the spectrum disorder, I learned he had recently had a full physical, but there were still many unknowns. Environmental allergies were involved and he took a prescribed medication for them. My questions were: What about food allergies? What about vision, hearing, or some other medical issue that might be at work? Does the medication he is taking for allergies make his behavioral problems worse? Has he been evaluated for learning disabilities? Are the behaviors he exhibits due to a traumatic event? Are the behaviors witnessed across environments or does he do better in certain situations?

After each question there was little response from the aunt. Probing, I asked how the term "spectrum disorder" had come up regarding this child. I learned it had been mentioned by one school professional but not someone able to make a formal diagnosis. In essence, no one knew for sure what was going on with this child. There were just some behaviors that looked like something we had a name for. Guessing is never the right response when a child is in need.

I suggested that before the aunt or other family member did anything, some important steps needed to be taken, and it would be necessary to backtrack and start at the beginning. The recommendations I offered apply to anyone who suspects or has been told about developmental, learning, attention, and physical and/or behavior issues related to their child.

Start with the obvious, ruling out anything you possibly can.

Drawing information from across environments and making connections between behavior and environment can be crucial to finding the right answers to help your child. For example, allergies can affect hearing and other physical systems, causing children to feel sick, miss school, and/or be inattentive and disrupted in school. It is important to rule out allergies and treat them if they exist before you pursue testing and treatment for learning disabilities. You could spend thousands of dollars and end up with a misdiagnosis and an invasive treatment related to learning or attention, when what needed to be addressed was a dietary change or allergy treatment. Symptoms masking the true problem can be alleviated by ruling out hearing, vision, and health issues before assuming a learning or attention issue is at work.

Make sure you enter into a conversation with any professional armed with as much information as possible. Being prepared with test results and related information can ensure you will get the best information from the person you are consulting. You can save time and money and even prevent misdiagnosis by ruling out the obvious.

7 Steps to Help You Get Started

The following list of recommendations provides a road map to help you get started.

1. *Create a family history including health, learning, behavioral, and emotional traits among family members.*

2. Create a living history of your child's life so far.

Information gathered from a family or child's history can be used to assist others in helping your child. The intention is not to draw negative conclusions from history but to look at differences and similarities to determine origin and patterns, so a proper diagnosis can be made and appropriate treatment can be found.

One of the reasons for creating a child's history is to think about the onset of particular behaviors and learning patterns. Knowing when something started often helps us to determine how to respond to it. Looking for the onset of a particular issue is important, but it's equally important to look for patterns. Does your child always exhibit this behavior or just in certain circumstances? Does everyone notice this about your child or just certain people? What precipitates this behavior, if anything? What causes the behavior (i.e., is there a trigger)? What connections can you make between setting (place), method (teacher, curriculum), intake (food, light, temperature), and response (reaction from child)?

When creating the history of your child, concentrate on positive aspects as much as possible. Questions to ask include:
- What does this child do well?
- What type of environment works best for him or her?
- What makes this child happy?
- What hobbies or activities does this child gravitate toward?
- What people (personality style and method) seem to work well with this child?
- What strategies are in place and work well to combat challenging behaviors?

Now ask those same questions from the opposite perspective. Example: What does this child struggle with?

If your child is old enough to speak and/or communicate, ask questions during learning and play time. By asking about his or her "thinking" process you will learn about your child's preferences and learning style. When asking these questions consider all settings including home, school, church, childcare, relatives' homes, friends' homes, sports activities, and other settings where the child learns and plays.

3. *Obtain a comprehensive vision evaluation.*

4. *Obtain a comprehensive hearing evaluation.*

5. *Obtain a comprehensive speech evaluation.*

6. *Obtain a comprehensive physical evaluation including blood sugar, anemia, allergies, thyroid, and endocrine functioning.*

I always suggest parents seek evaluations from board certified physicians specializing in a particular area of study such as vision, hearing, etc. The tests at school are only a screening tool not a complete evaluation. Even if your child passes this screening there still may be an issue. See a specialist before you rule out particular problems regarding eyes, ears, and health. In addition be aware that some allergy testing may not be sensitive enough to detect a slight allergy to food or other allergens. If you suspect an allergy exists, but a test does not reveal the allergy, you may need to seek more sensitive testing to be sure.

7. *Obtain comprehensive testing for IQ, aptitude, learning styles, learning disabilities (usually an IQ test is a part of this testing) including dyslexia and other language-based disorders, attention deficit/hyperactivity disorder, and sensory processing issues.*

Be aware that anything can cause behavior change. Environmental allergies, teaching method, furniture arrangement, schedule, peer group, or setting can change how a child operates. In addition, food, medication, and even vitamins can affect your child's behavior and learning. Therefore, it is important to monitor your child to determine what changes occur in behavior and learning when a new setting or a new substance (food or chemical) is introduced.

When looking for help be sure to screen practitioners and specialists carefully. Anyone can put up a shingle, but not everyone is qualified to evaluate a child for learning or physical issues. In addition, even the most well-meaning and highly qualified doctor or specialist can have an agenda or offer advice based on limited information. Your trusted family doctor may be able to diagnose ADHD, but may not know how to create a comprehensive plan for treatment. For example he or she may offer medication as the solution when, in fact, there should be other components of the treatment plan to achieve the best results. Consult with those you trust, but understand that any given professional isn't going to have all the answers and shouldn't have the last word on diagnosis and treatment.

Our bodies and minds are complicated creations. Be cautious about "quick fixes" whether they involve medication, supplements, or methods. I have yet to see a quick fix be a total solution. Often, the "quick fix" will provide a mechanism for getting through but won't be a "cure" or long-term answer. Sometimes a quick fix can actually cause more problems because you end up treating a symptom rather than addressing the root cause.

Even if you are really desperate, be willing to look at the least invasive and most natural approach whenever possible, and use this approach in combination with a complete treatment plan. A treatment plan should take into consideration a holistic view of the child including mental, emotional, and physical health as well as learning and behavior. In addition this plan should provide strategies and methods across environments.

Record Keeping

Keep a portfolio of work from each year containing report cards, special projects, a writing sample from the beginning, middle, and end of the year, and at least one assignment related to reading progress. This information is not only a fun way for kids to look back on a particular year, but it provides a record of performance at any given grade level. Individuals involved with evaluating your child can review past work to provide a basis for comparison if there is a sudden change in performance or need for evaluation.

Though a school file is important, it is often incomplete. To ensure that you can be the best advocate possible—even if you change schools or academic setting—keep a record of the results of all medical evaluations and school evaluations. This information, along with your child's portfolio and historical data, provides a more comprehensive view of your child and his or her academic performance.

Often confidential records are released to medical personnel, not to individuals, and schools may be skittish about releasing a school file or records within a file, even to a parent. Though you may encounter resistance when you request the information, you have a right to it. If you are persistent, you will likely obtain the information but may have to sign a release form and hand-carry sensitive paperwork as opposed to having it mailed or faxed.

Keep all medical records and other diagnostic-related materials at least until a student graduates from college. If you have a copy of current tests (usually tests are considered current within three years of testing), your child should not have to be retested to receive services when moving from one district to another or when you apply for services at the college level.

Take Care When You Share

Consider what you share, how you share it, and with whom you share it. When I was 18, I traveled to a local school to give a talk. Parents were invited to this particular meeting. Following my speech a parent pushed through the crowd with her son in tow and an intense expression on her face. Having just finished saying good-bye to the person in front of her, I was surprised to hear this mother announce in a loud voice, "My kid is failing school and has the same thing you do. What do I do about him?"

The "kid" who stood just behind his mom was clearly not hearing impaired. By his desperate look, slumped shoulders, and downcast eyes I knew this was not the first time his mother had "unintentionally" spoken about his "issues" to everyone within earshot. I was devastated for him. I knew if she was willing to speak to a stranger and use those terms, whatever she said in the home, to someone on the phone, or in a school conference was probably much worse. Sometimes, in an effort to help, we do much more harm with our words.

Having come from a living situation where I was exposed to more information than my little mind could handle, I tend to be conservative when it comes to anything my children see or hear. I also am careful when sharing—even about my own life. Aside from the fact that my kids know my parents are married to other people, they don't know about my history in school or anything else related to my home life. I am not keeping secrets. I am being a conscientious parent, considering and weighing what I think my children need to know against my need to ramble. I want my children to be free of any bondage from my past. I can teach them lessons without spilling my guts. I also am careful about what I say when they aren't in the room. Little ears are always listening. I also don't say things to other people by phone or in person that I don't want them to hear, not even if I spell it or speak in code. My rule is that if it isn't going to help my children be healthier or well adjusted, it shouldn't be said. If I need to speak about a situation, I do so with the door shut to avoid burdening my children or creating unnecessary worry or fear about themselves, their physical or intellectual development, or our family's well-being.

Protect your children from hurtful and irrelevant information. In the end, it's not where kids end up but where they start that is most important. Kids may need to be aware of their diagnosis so they can advocate for themselves and even understand that they are different but not bad. What isn't helpful is talking about negative outcomes and cynical projections. None of this will help your child reach his or her potential. Anything shared with a child should also be done in an age-appropriate way so the child isn't overwhelmed or unable to grasp what he or she is being told and how it will affect his or her life.

Protecting your child also means you have to consider everything you say and to whom you say it. Whispered discussion, and even the most discreet conversations, can be overheard and misinterpreted. Furthermore, well-meaning family or extended family and friends can unintentionally give your child information that is not necessary to share or make projections based on early evidence that is not relevant for your child to hear. Our words are analogous to feathers in the wind. We can't take them back and cannot always control where they land. Put great thought into how, when, and with whom you share.

Education Law 101

Many parents have told me negative stories about how their children didn't receive special education services, did not receive services in a timely fashion, received inadequate services, and/or had to fight to get the services. Though I am totally sympathetic to the frustration of parents who encounter challenges, I try to stay positive about public education and view where we are now through the perspective of history. Not so long ago kids could be institutionalized or kept out of school due to disabilities and handicapping conditions. So while there is still much work to do and problems exist, we have come a long way.

In 1975 Public Law 94-142 (Education of All Handicapped Children Act) was signed by President Ford. This law has been adjusted and changed over the years and even has a different name: Individuals with Disabilities Education Act. Though the name has changed, the original principles of the law remain the same. Under the law every child is guaranteed a free and appropriate education in the least restrictive environment and the right to due process.

Prior to 1975 millions of children and adolescents were not in school due to handicapping conditions. Students were often institutionalized, educated in "residential schools," or at the very least separated in self-contained classrooms (having little or no interaction with other students) in their neighborhood schools. There was a pervasive feeling that "disabled" kids would not benefit from socialization or education with "normal" kids. PL-94-142 changed all that.

Now we have the Americans with Disabilities Act to protect individuals with disabilities in terms of housing, employment, and access to public services. We also have Section 504 of the Rehabilitation Act, signed into law in 1973. This law protects anyone from discrimination in a public setting. In search of a way to address the needs of students who otherwise didn't fit under the legal umbrella of "disabilities," Section 504 provides for accommodations for students experiencing "other" conditions such as ADHD.

The changes that have occurred in availability of services, and how we deliver those services, is remarkable. We moved from exclusion, to self-contained, to mainstreamed, to inclusion models in less than a generation. As exciting as it is to see this kind of positive growth, it has not come without growing pains.

If you have experienced frustration with the system of special education, here are some possible reasons:

- Due to the diligence of parents, lawmakers, and advocacy groups, laws changed. However, when it was agreed that everyone deserved an education, it might have been wise to determine how much this was going to cost. Schools were left scrambling, thanks to wide-open words and phrases such as "free," "appropriate," and "least restrictive" written into the law with no specific guidelines governing services provided for specific cases. As you might expect, it wasn't long before lawyers got involved and soon court cases were rampant. Because there was no way to define legal terms such as "least restrictive" for each individual student, the law attempted to define which services would be given to certain students and set a precedent for what others could expect.

- Lawsuits are an expensive way to determine how we teach students. It would be better if due process and mediation could result in a response that satisfied all parties. Because that doesn't always happen, the issue winds up in court. In some cases there are legitimate requests from parents contained in a lawsuit. Of course parents want the best for their children. But when you study a given budget and know it has to cover the needs of all students, you can see the problem. There isn't enough money to provide the level of service every parent wants and, in some cases, even the level of service that is necessary. Therefore, even the most legitimate claim in a lawsuit can appear unreasonable when

it means one student's needs will be provided for, but services for another student will be cut.

- In many cases, lawsuits changed the way particular services
  were delivered or how many services were offered, so the
  cost of special education and bureaucracy associated with it
  skyrocketed. While the services provided to one student as
  dictated by a lawsuit might make perfect sense, the cost in
  some cases was so onerous that other special education and
  even regular education students would be denied services
  or programs because there was no more money to provide
  specialists, assistive technology, and other forms of special
  education support without breaking the bank.

- As we have made changes in programs and service-delivery
  models (self-contained to inclusion), we haven't done a
  good job helping teachers and administrators make the
  transition. Once again, there are no perfect guidelines, just
  the spirit of the law as our guide. Many teachers have been
  frustrated because they feel unprepared to teach students
  with special needs in a regular educational environment.

- The bureaucracy associated with special education is unbe-
  lievable. Paperwork is never-ending. In some cases teachers
  spend more time doing paperwork than working with children. Some individuals actually leave the profession
  because the nature of the job has changed so significantly
  due to the paper trail required by law for each student.

- Because special services for disabled students are required
  under the law, but there are no universal rules on how to
  implement them, programs may vary even within a school

district. Parents who move often find themselves negotiating for services in one district that were a given in another.

- There is no getting around the human element. Because the system of special education—and education in general—is run by humans, errors will occur. Well-intentioned people make mistakes, tests are not always right, programs aren't always implemented correctly, and budgets are tight. Acknowledging this means you can be dogged in your quest to help your child but should be willing to offer mercy when honest mistakes happen or the wheels of progress move slowly.

What You Should Know About Special Education

Again, your child has the right to a free and appropriate education in public schools provided in the least restrictive environment. The least restrictive environment is not always the regular education classroom. There are times where a student will do better if some services are provided in a smaller setting. This is called a pull-out program or learning center approach. In this case, the separation is done to benefit the child, not to exclude him or her.

Note: The following outline regarding the special education process applies when a learning disability or academic performance issue exists. Children with physical disabilities have a slightly different process because their condition may not involve learning and would likely have been diagnosed by a doctor in early life.

- Referral: A parent consults with the child's teacher about an issue related to school performance. A teacher can also consult with a parent about a child and suggest that a problem exists. Note: Referrals can be made by other school personnel, but typically the process is started between teacher and parent.

• Testing: If agreement is reached between the parent and teacher that an issue exists, a referral is made to the school psychologist. Using the information from parent and teacher, the school psychologist will administer certain tests to establish intellectual functioning and learning ability. Note: A child cannot be tested without a parent's permission.

• Evaluation: The findings of the tests are presented in a meeting. This meeting usually includes the child's teacher, the school psychologist, the school's special education teacher, and the child's parents. This team is often called the Multidisciplinary Team. Recommendations are made in this meeting regarding whether or not the child qualifies for services. If the child qualifies for services, the parent needs to agree that services can be delivered.

• IEP: An individualized education plan is created by the special education teacher and/or the school psychologist. The IEP contains background information, test results, diagnosis, recommendations, short- and long-term goals for addressing the special need(s) of the child, and the time frame estimated for accomplishing those objectives. The IEP is presented to parents and discussed in depth. If parents feel comfortable with the contents of the document, the IEP is implemented and the student receives services.

At the time of the IEP meeting, parents can request changes to the content in the IEP document. Once in place the IEP stands as the legal document requiring service delivery. Parents typically attend a meeting at least once a year to discuss the student's progress based on services provided. The IEP is updated to reflect an objective that has been met and new goals to be achieved. If further testing is required to determine if goals have been met or if the student has overcome the learning issue that prompted the IEP, the existing IEP will reflect this information.

What You Should Know About Testing

You have the right to have your child tested at no cost for specific learning and behavior-related issues. Understand that the timetable depends on important factors such as the number of students waiting to be tested and how many personnel in the school or district are qualified to adminster the tests. It will take time to get the testing done, but the time should not be excessive (more than six months). For best results, ask for a specific timetable at the time of referral.

All tests become a part of the child's permanent record. If your preference is to go to an outside source for testing, you can choose whether the tests will become a part of your child's permanent record. To receive services in a district, though, the tests from an outside source must meet the standards of those that would have been given by the district. They must be administered by a qualified professional and must become part of the child's record.

After your child has been tested, you can ask for a retest if you disagree with the results. Getting retested seldom is done immediately. A waiting period of months or even a year may be required. If you disagree with the results of the tests offered by your school or district, you can go to an outside source at your expense.

Special education qualification guidelines vary from district to district, school to school, and year to year. These guidelines can be arbitrary at times and may shift based on population size of the school, funding (local, state, and federal), new and old budget issues (surplus and debt), and legal issues such as lawsuits and government mandates. Because the criteria for entrance into special education can vary, there are times when a student who might have qualified the year before (if he or she had been tested) wouldn't qualify the next year. If your child is already being served, he or she wouldn't be dropped from service based on new criteria, but new cases are subject to the new criteria for enrollment in special services. This information is important to note because if your child does not qualify for special education in a given school/district, it does not mean your child is not experiencing learning (behavior, etc.) problems and does not need special services. If you feel your child is experiencing problems related to learning (or other issues) don't hesitate to advocate for further testing and necessary services. You may also want to explore outside testing and support services if the "wait time" for such services in your school or district is too long.

If your child doesn't qualify for special education in a particular school year, you can ask for your student to be retested. Again, a waiting period may be required before retesting is done. If you do not wish to wait for retesting, you can opt to have testing performed outside the school. Be sure any tests you get from an outside source will be accepted by the district.

It is essential to go to a reputable source for testing, and the best way to find a testing facility is through a state or national association. I contacted our state association for children and adults with learning disabilities when I was tested as an adult. In some cases the association has testing facilities, and sometimes they will offer referrals to other reputable organizations. Outside testing can be expensive. Be sure to ask for sliding scale fees, scholarships, and state aid.

If your child is having difficulty, but he or she doesn't qualify for special education at your local public school, you could explore several options:

- Continue advocating for your child to receive in-class support from his or her regular education teacher and supplement with outside services such as tutoring.
- Explore the possibility of getting a waiver into another school in your local district or a neighboring district that may have smaller classroom size or other services to accommodate your child's needs.
- In some cases even though a child does not qualify in one district, he or she could qualify in another. It might be worthwhile to consider a waiver, but don't make a move to another district before asking a lot of questions to confirm services based on your child's existing public school record.
- Explore private schools, boarding schools, charter schools, homeschooling, or homeschooling cooperatives as alternatives.

Know the Law. Know Your Rights

If someone at school suggests your child is experiencing a specific learning, behavioral, or physical issue, you can disagree, decline testing, and opt out of receiving special services.

If you choose to receive special services but disagree with the services provided, the setting for the services, or any aspect of service delivery, you can request a meeting with the multidisciplinary team (the group of people who work with your child to deliver services) to discuss the situation. If you cannot get the issue resolved in a satisfactory way, you can take your grievance to the next level of due process and request mediation. If you still feel the issue has not been resolved and you have exhausted all options related to due process, you can take legal action. While pursuing a legal remedy in some cases is necessary, it is important to investigate support services and financial aid if you choose this course of action.

Be honest but cautious. Anything you say during a meeting at the school level can become part of the permanent record.

Sitting across from "the experts" can be intimidating and emotional. If you have a trusted individual and/or professional who can help you through this process, I highly recommend it. You know yourself. If bringing someone with you would create more tension, obviously it is not a good idea. Don't bring people to a meeting who will muddy the water, become hostile, or talk too much. Choose your support individual or group wisely. Make sure this person is knowledgeable if he or she will speak on your behalf at any time and will have your best interests and the best interests of your child in mind. Possibilities could include the child's other parent, caregiver, relative, doctor, member of an advocacy group, and so on.

When you are armed with detailed information about your child and test results that rule out particular issues, you will be a much better advocate. In the early stages of referral you may not have had a chance to have particular testing done or have gathered historical data. In any meeting about your child, don't hesitate to hold off on decision making until you have had a chance to gather this information. Time is of the essence, but if you can gather information that will help others more appropriately diagnose and treat your child, then your time will be well spent on a fact-finding mission before any testing or treatment is pursued.

Due process is your right as a parent. You can request a hearing regarding your child's testing, diagnosis, placement, and service delivery model. If you feel your child is being denied services, has been given the wrong services or inadequate services, and/or if you wish to contest any issue related to your child's school experience—such as placement—you can request the opportunity for further consideration. Typically, mediation will take place first. If the issue cannot be resolved, a hearing will be held. If resolution cannot be found, the case can become a legal issue and move into the judicial system.

Working Within the System

Stephanie sat in the back row of an auditorium in Palm Beach, Florida. Though I didn't know her, for some reason she looked like an important person, and I wondered if she was a dignitary who had not been introduced. When she approached me after my talk, I was pretty sure she would say hello and be on her way. Instead, she waited until I had spoken to everyone, then offered to have lunch with me. After small talk over salad at a local restaurant, Stephanie told me her story.

Several months after a traumatic, late-term stillbirth, she found herself pregnant with twins. Once again, there were complications. The babies were born very early. One baby was dead, one baby had cerebral palsy, and Stephanie nearly died from blood loss.

After gathering herself from this devastating loss, Stephanie poured herself into her role as mother. Early predictions about her daughter were not good. If doctors were right, Jordan would not walk or talk—ever. This prognosis was simply not acceptable to Stephanie. Without being unreasonable in her expectations, she hoped Jordan would one day take a few steps and maybe even ride a bike.

Realizing the level of professional care Jordan would need to be able to progress, Stephanie left nothing to chance. Jordan was enrolled in early intervention programs offered by her local school district and attended physical and other forms of therapy to improve mobility. If there was a method or therapy out there to help, Stephanie searched to find it.

Regarding the public schools, right away Stephanie noticed flaws in the system. Certain services that should have been provided weren't. Programs that should have been available were not available or were offered at an insufficient level.

If she had chosen to, Stephanie could have looked for a private school or chosen some other avenue of education. Instead, she sent her daughter to her neighborhood public school. She knew that public schools can and do work, but nothing is perfect. Never one to stand by and hope for the best, Stephanie intended to work within the system to make it better. Volunteering in the school, joining committees working toward disabilities awareness as well as teacher appreciation, being active in the community as a speaker and advocate, Stephanie committed herself to making a difference. While dealing with the physical and educational needs of her daughter, she also took part in political action committees and advocacy groups to ensure that public schools have the proper funding to provide the level of service necessary for each student. In the end, what she is doing not only elevates the level of education her daughter will receive, it raises the level of education all kids will receive.

No doubt she is tired at the end of the day, but Stephanie can look at the little girl Jordan has become—the one who rides a bike—and know her investment in time and energy was well placed.

It is so easy to throw stones, be cynical, and walk away. I would never suggest we sacrifice our children's best interests for the greater good by staying in a situation that isn't working, but like a stone skipping across water, your investment in public schools could have a ripple effect and touch the lives of generations of children and their families.

On its face, volunteering at your child's school would appear to do the obvious: help the school. But research shows that when kids see their parents at school helping (in any capacity), they get the message that school is important and, therefore, they are important. When you volunteer at school, you discover another benefit. You develop deeper relationships with teachers, administrators, and support staff. These relationships will serve you when or if your child requires special services or special attention. Interacting with people and serving at the school is like building a bank account of "cultural capital." Cultural capital is the trust and knowledge built between two people. The more you have of it, the better interactions work. Having history with another person usually leads to better communication, even if we don't understand where the other person is coming from. There is a greater willingness to listen and also to forgive when we disagree.

As accurate as it may be to view education as a right, public schools are expensive and are only as effective as the support they receive from parents, the community, and government. Whether or not you are a parent of a special-needs child, I hope you choose to get involved in some way to support schools. If you need to opt out of the public school system to get the proper assistance and learning environment for your child, don't opt out of being involved in any form of education reform and improvement.

The simple act of volunteering can make a big difference. Opportunities exist before school, during school, and after school. If you cannot volunteer at the school building, ask teachers and administrators if there is work that can be done at home. Participate in groups and associations whenever possible. Activities and meetings offered through organizations such as the PTA will provide you with information about the school and help you to create relationships with other parents. Parent networking is a great way to learn about services and programs available at school or in the community.

Early Intervention

Early intervention is so important because the sooner we offer assistance, the more likely it is that a child will succeed. In the early years, and even beyond, we are our children's best advocates. To successfully advocate for your child, you need to come from a place of knowledge.

Even in the early stages of life we need to be "case managers" of our children's growth and development. We need to look at movement, affect (emotional connection), reactions (hearing, seeing, and other senses), and sensory processing (reaction to stimuli and type of stimuli). Looking at simple things such as eye contact, reactions to loud and soft noises, and development of coordination, we can determine if our children are meeting standards for development. Development is on a continuum, so not every child will reach milestones at the same time as every other child, but there are windows during which we should see certain development markers attained. By staying tuned in to signals and signs—without being hypervigilant—we can look for anything out of the ordinary and pursue assistance if necessary.

Well before school starts, we can tap into a rich source of data about all areas of development by watching our children at play. Whether playing with other children or family members or playing on their own, children can give us lots of information about how they think, what their strengths are, how they relate to other people and their environment, how they are doing socially, and more.

To be certain your child is in line with basic standards of growth and development before he or she starts school, check with your pediatrician or local school district. Markers for development can help you identify your child's level and determine if a delay exists. If you notice any delays before your child enters school, you can look for early screening programs. If a problem is confirmed, your child can receive services through early intervention and enrichment programs for children birth to age three, available through state agencies, non-profit organizations, and public schools. When children enter school, their "readiness" for each grade level can be determined by checking state and/or district standards. If you suspect your child might be lagging behind grade level, talk with his or her teacher about the situation.

Advocating for Your Child

Just when I thought all my emotional kinks were worked out, I had kids. I flipped out over my first child's every scrape, bump, and negative experience. I was supposed to be his advocate, but I took everything personally and couldn't seem to get perspective. Michael's experiences in school, both good and bad, seasoned me. As his representative, I learned to be proactive and prepared to act in a positive way.

When I was little, my mom was friendly and brought brownies to try to influence people to help me. There were no existing laws to protect my placement in school, so she had to rely on chocolate and compliments. Times have changed, and though I still think sweets are a good way to start a conversation, they are not my only suggested strategy for advocating for your child.

If a problem arises in any setting, there are several things you can do to advocate for your child in a positive way.

- Pray about the situation before you say or do anything.
- Determine if the situation warrants action.
- Consider what action plan would be appropriate for the situation.
- If you have concerns, direct your comments only to the individual(s) involved.
- Do not involve a superior unless you cannot reach a resolution with the individual(s) concerned.
- Talk in person whenever possible, but be aware of time limitations.
- Use e-mail or letters to document conversations.
- Document everything, including the time and date of phone calls and the name of the person you spoke to, so you can refer to the information if you do not get a timely response.
- Be aware that writing can often sound abrupt. Make sure a letter or e-mail is direct but warm.
- Write down what you want to say, so anything you share in person will be coherent, nothing will be left out, and your remarks will be to the point.
- After writing your thoughts on paper, sleep on it. Sometimes when you awake and reread the information, you will no longer feel as deeply about something and can choose not to react.
- If you choose to send something in writing, critically look at your remarks to ensure what you have shared is factual and not emotional.
- Don't share anything unnecessary, either in writing or conversation. Stick to the issue.

- If you need to talk with someone, do not do so when the person is busy. Make an appointment for a time when everyone involved will be able to hear and attend to the topic.
- Respond only to important issues that directly impact your child.
- Ask questions and listen.
- Use language that is edifying.
- Have all the facts before making accusations.
- Frontload all discussions with positive remarks, if at all possible.
- Do not agree to anything on the spur of the moment. It is reasonable to request time to consider options and get a second opinion.
- Request a timetable for action.
- If a conflict arises that cannot be resolved between the two parties involved, request mediation through the school district or have the issue addressed by a higher authority in the organization.

Best Practices for Parents

When I was going to school to earn my teaching certificate, I learned about best practices, a set of methods teachers may employ to best meet the needs of all students. Best practices include offering multiple ways for students to demonstrate what they have learned, not just through written tests. They include the many ways students can learn information, tailored to a variety of learning styles and environmental preferences. It is nearly impossible to make every lesson accessible to every learner, but you can adjust, create accommodations, and be creative with material and lesson planning to help all students learn.

Most of my own teachers did not hold master's degrees in education or special education, yet they were outstanding educators. They applied principles of good teaching combined with a willingness to adjust their approaches. In other words, they were creative in method and curriculum in order to meet my needs. The good news is the "best practices" my teachers employed did not exclude the needs of regular education students. These teaching practices were sound and effective for all students.

As with excellent teaching, some simple and effective parenting principles work for all children, including those with special needs.

Back to Basics

If you are facing obstacles as a parent, I strongly suggest you watch a TV show called *Supernanny*. Within a few minutes you will feel so much better about your situation. While you may think there is no hope for some of the families featured on the show because the children's behavior is so extreme, the nanny somehow comes to the rescue with effective solutions every week.

Supernanny is a woman named Jo. Though she is relatively young, her English accent makes her seem both endearing and wise beyond her years as she addresses behavior, attention, and learning issues. It's interesting to me that the solutions Jo provides are, well, so obvious. Each week a new family is treated to a basic class in positive parenting. Parents are told to spend time with their children, make eye contact when giving praise, show interest in play and other positive behaviors, and provide specific praise for good behavior. While it's not exactly revolutionary, this approach demonstrates that a simple solution can work. The solutions are basic, but they require a commitment on the parents' part, as well as their time and willingness to engage with their kids and provide consistency. Therein lies the beauty and the message. We go a long way to find answers to our parenting challenges, but often the solution is right in front of us.

When faced with challenges, we can easily get stuck and become too tired and frustrated to find a way out. Sometimes going back to the basics is the best way to regain our footing so we can find a solution. Basic solutions we'll explore next in more detail include: building a foundation of faith; character education; time and attention; positive discipline; structure and organizational skills; and finding strengths.

Building a Foundation of Faith

I recently spoke by phone to a friend who was over the edge with worry. Her wonderful daughter was making a wrong decision, and my friend felt she could do nothing to stop it. On the verge of tears and nearly hysterical, this parent was out of control with worry and fear. In the middle of her outpouring, I stopped her and asked, "What is the one thing we can always do, the most powerful tool we have as parents?"

The other end of the line was quiet.

"What do we have control over?" I continued.

She said, "What we say and what we do."

I said, "But what if there is nothing more we can say or do to help or redirect our child?"

Softly she answered, "We can pray."

Even as a Christian, fear of the unknown had set this mother spinning, exhausting herself talking and doing. The problem continued. Frantic and overwhelmed, she had forgotten that we have physical limitations. Sometimes there is nothing we can "do" (through action or talk) to improve a situation. The only card we can play anytime and anywhere is one that will have the greatest results: prayer.

I rarely learned a Bible verse, but I knew what love looked like. I didn't have any friends, my dad was not in our home, but I had a Friend and Father in Jesus. Faith was free, but it was the most important gift I was ever given.

I cannot think of anything more important in parenting than teaching children about God and faith. When faith is your foundation, there really is no end to the possibilities. Faith on your part means there is always hope, obstacles can be overcome, and giving up is not an option. Faith in God can teach your child about mercy, forgiveness, discipline, higher authority, service, destiny, eternity, purpose, and that even "the least of these" is important. What more crucial lessons are there?

These are some basic principles for building a foundation of faith:

- Give your child more than the world can. Teach him or her about God. He is the most powerful friend your child will ever know and the only one he or she will ever need.

- Read the Bible and pray together.

- Get involved in a Bible-based church that can offer support, encouragement, and sound teaching for you and your family.
- Look for teachable moments when there is an opportunity to address problems with prayer and offer biblical truths and lessons to everyday situations.
- Provide an example of faith for children by giving praise even during difficult times and praying even when the situation looks bleak.
- Remind children of prayers answered and even those answered "no" or "wait." There are lessons in each.

Character Education

It is exciting to see more and more schools include character education lessons as part of health and life skills curriculums. The problem is, when social pressure is intense, character traits such as integrity can seem antiquated and hard to apply. The best way to teach character education is to embed it in teaching about faith. Our children learn it from the most important people in their lives—parents and caregivers.

Character education in the home can be simple. First, kids need to know what character is. I define it for children in the following way: Character is a set of traits. Character traits include things like integrity, honor, and courage. I suggest kids think of character as a muscle that is strengthened every time we use it. I explain that the character muscle can be used in easy situations, but it will only get a little stronger because it is easier to act honorably when it isn't very hard to. The muscle gets really strong when we use character traits in difficult situations where we might be afraid to defend our faith or stick up for a friend being bullied. As we demonstrate character in all situations, especially difficult ones, our muscle grows strong. As with muscle memory, our character muscle will soon react without even having to think about it. Soon we can weather difficult storms like peer pressure without bending or breaking in the wind.

Talk about character with your children. Demonstrate character in the home. Let your children watch you face struggles with faith—not fear—and life pressures with honor. Over time they will learn to apply these lessons to their own lives, and the practice of acting with character will become second nature.

Time and Attention

When I was in graduate school, a very interesting study was discussed in one of my classes. Two groups of kindergarten-age children were observed in the study. One group was paid money to play with toys. The other group was not paid to play. The researchers found that the children paid to play eventually lost interest in play. The findings suggest there is something inherently motivating about play, but when paid to do the exact play activities, children turn their attention to money. Children begin to think they are playing for the money, and it becomes much more like a job. The joy is robbed from the activity because money shifted the focus.

Think about how many times your children say, "Look at me, look at me." They want your attention, your focus, and your approval. When we shift their attention to "things" to make up for the time we can't (or won't) give them, eventually they view "things" as important. Though kids may think they want things, they are, in fact, settling for the only thing we offered. Eventually the toy (thing) gets abandoned and they wonder why they feel empty. We paid them to play, then wondered why they lost interest in spending time with us.

There is no substitute for time (no toy, no activity is as important), so it is essential to find ways to restructure our lives so we have time to give our children. Remove distractions and omit even service activities to be with them. With work and other demands in our lives, quantity of time may be less, but the quality can be more if you plan for the special occasion and carve out time to do simple but meaningful things. By doing this you show kids that even when time is limited, they are a priority.

Positive Discipline

As a parent of four children, I've had my moments of pure exasperation when seeing one of my darling children push the boundary line just to confirm who is in charge. But I know my child's future depends on my response to both the good and bad behavior he or she exhibits. I want to try to preempt wrong behaviors by having a positive discipline plan, one that builds on the strengths of my children and sets the tone for a consistent and fair response when my kids don't do the right thing.

There isn't a one-size-fits all approach to discipline, and you really have to look at each child as an individual to know what will be most effective. Still, there are principles and strategies to consider in every case.

When you spend time with your children, you may find your attention actually helps to reduce wrong behaviors. More family time provides opportunity for character education and faith lessons too, helping to reduce the need for discipline. Even with preventive measures in place, such as a solid foundation of faith and increased family-time opportunities, there will always be the need for a positive action plan in terms of discipline.

A positive plan for discipline should be:

- Clear: everyone knows the consequences for bad behavior and the consequences for good behavior.
- Consistent: the same consequences always apply.
- Individualized: considerate of age, intellectual development, and emotional/personality style.
- Preemptive: focused on teaching and praising good behavior rather than looking for or waiting for bad behavior to occur or assuming it will.
- Positive: using words of praise and redirection, eye contact, and reassuring touch.

We spend a lot of time telling kids what not to do. Kids who have "special needs" often think the only thing they are good at is getting in trouble. Teaching children and modeling what to do, how to do it, and when to do it will help ensure their success.

You can highlight the positive nature of a child's differences to increase that child's positive view of himself or herself. For instance, show how excess energy can be a plus by allowing the child to be your helper, or engage him or her in a sport where excess energy is needed.

Along with a plan for positive discipline, consider how you can prepare your child for success by offering specific praise, rewards for good behavior, and an opportunity to work in the child's area(s) of strength.

Suggestions for redirecting behavior include:

• Target one behavior in need of change at a time.

• Demonstrate and model the type of behavior you want your child to exhibit.

• Allow your child to role play positive behaviors to practice appropriate responses.

• Offer specific and immediate praise regarding even the smallest positive behavior. This will cause a child to internalize the effect he or she had on the outcome and internalize the behavior.

• Do the same thing, at the same time each day, to help the child focus on the task embedded in a schedule. This will result in habits being learned faster.

• Use a "token" system rather than monetary rewards to motivate. Money tends to undermine motivation even toward tasks kids enjoy. A token system could include no-cost options such as certificates enabling children to spend time with you having simple fun such as watching a movie or playing a game. Other ideas include tokens to be exchanged for small toys or trinkets in a "store" that you create.

• Chart successes to enable kids to see their progress. Visual markers allow children to see that they are moving toward goals.

Structure and Order

Children, especially those experiencing special needs, will always benefit from structure and order. When you are experiencing a learning or behavior issue, it often feels like the world is one big set of surprises. Because you feel overwhelmed by internal "noise" (systems inside the body that operate differently) and external "noise" (sound, movement, and other forms of intake to the senses), it is hard to attend to what you want to. It's even hard to know what is important to attend to. By taking out unknowns such as when to wake up, what to do when you wake up, and so on, kids can concentrate on the unexpected things they can't anticipate. Everyone can benefit from the concept of structure without having creativity squelched or learning style disregarded. The idea is to develop systems that work best for each child, so getting through the day becomes more predictable and less complicated.

These recommendations can help you improve structure and increase order:

- Provide an orderly living environment.
- Demonstrate the importance of habits and routines by implementing them in your own life.
- Don't expect children to order their world in the same way you do. Develop habits and routines that work best for each.
- Develop habits that together become routines. Routines take the guesswork out of what to do, when to do it, and how to do it. Focus on one aspect of the day—such as morning preparation for school—and break it down into simple sets of tasks (get up and make the bed, for example) for each part of the routine.

- Use checklists in order of the tasks to be completed to confirm each task has been done.
- Continue the use of a checklist until each task becomes a habit and the habits become a routine.

Be prepared to demonstrate and teach (in small steps) each task within a routine to ensure children can successfully complete each task.

- Give specific and immediate praise for tasks completed and redirect when tasks are not completed or the task is not completed in the order necessary for the habits to become a routine.
- Practice the routine when there is no time pressure.

Organizational Skills

I cannot believe I am about to say this, but here goes. Being organized is necessary. If you are creative, global, or, like me, organizationally challenged, you probably want to throw something at me. I know, I know. I was born without the organizational chip too. It doesn't come naturally to me to do anything in a straight line. I have learned to be organized out of necessity but have adjusted systems and methods to best fit the way I learn and my personality style.

Being organized doesn't have to require changing an innate personality style to achieve conformity. Organization patterns can be individualized to best fit you and your child. Simple habits will form into routines resulting in reduced stress, less wasted energy, and more time to enjoy life and creative pursuits.

Develop a system of organization one skill at a time by

addressing one problem area at a time, working from smaller to larger. For instance, rather than organizing a whole room, organize one drawer.

Here are five easy steps for approaching an organization task:

1. Establish the task's relevance. How will this help you?
2. Establish sub-tasks. What are we going to do?
3. Determine the order of sub-tasks. How are we going to do it?
4. Explain how to do the sub-tasks.
5. Create a checklist for sub-tasks so the child can be sure he or she has completed all the sub-tasks.

Remember to always organize according to need.

1. Put away things you don't need.
2. Throw away or give away things you will never use.
3. The items you use should be placed in such a way that you can easily get them. They should be arranged according to how and when you use each item. Try the following:
   - Place similar things together.
   - Color code or stack according to size or shape.
   - Designate locations in the room where certain activities take place. Provide proper-sized storage for the items located in that area to help kids put things away in the right place and in the right order.
   - Realize that while planners, calendars, and other organizational and assistive devices can be helpful, they require instruction and monitoring to be effective.

Finding Solutions by Focusing on Strengths

A mother recently approached me after a speech and explained that her son experienced learning disabilities and had been struggling in school for many years. She said, "He knows strategies that he can use to help himself. It seems like he will use them for a little while, then he will begin failing again."

I asked a simple question: "When, if ever, does he do well in school?"

She surprised me. I thought she might say "never" or "rarely."

Instead, she replied, "He only does well during the first quarter of the year."

This boy, now in early high school, had a pattern. I asked her, "What goes on during the first quarter of the year that might be different from the rest of the year?"

Without hesitation she said, "Soccer."

"That is really interesting," I said. "You would think playing a sport and going to school might be difficult for him, but something about soccer season really works for him."

She said, "Yeah, I think he works better when his schedule is full because he is forced to structure himself."

Knowing the boy had learning issues, I asked if he struggled with attention or hyperactivity issues.

She said, "Oh, yes! He is very hyperactive." She then hung her head as if the situation seemed hopeless.

I thought the solution seemed easy. I asked, "Have you ever looked into year-round soccer through select teams and indoor leagues?"

She said, "No," but the light went on in her eyes.

I continued, "What if, knowing he does well during soccer season, you made soccer season every season? It could be he is more active during soccer season and able to deal with his energy and attention issues, or it could be that busyness prevents distraction. It is hard to know for sure, but something is working for him when he combines school and soccer."

This wonderful mom had tried so hard to help her son. She did the right thing early. She knew her son had a lot of energy and got him into soccer, but when failure at school became the biggest problem, the "successes" this boy had were overlooked as a possible solution. Soon the problem was all that could be seen, and any pattern of positive behavior was lost.

Looking at a problem for too long can cause us to only see the problem. The solution might be so easy, but we just can't see it. When you are facing a challenging behavior or learning issue with your child, look away from the problem and focus on your child's strengths for answers.

The following recommendations should help you focus on a child's strengths:

- Watch and listen to your child as he or she operates in different settings and works on different activities. This will help you understand your child's style, strengths, and even weaknesses, so you can teach him or her to work smarter within individual areas of strength.
- If your child is old enough to talk and is able to communicate, ask him or her to talk out loud while at work. This type of "talking through" will often enable you to see how

your child processes information and help you understand why he or she makes certain choices.

- Identify what your child does well and explain in detail these strengths to your child.
- Make sure your child knows specifically what he or she does well and can communicate those strengths to the people around him or her.
- Help children take what they are good at and apply those skills to other areas of their lives.
- Find ways to connect new information to what the child does well. The concept of connecting science (new) with soccer (familiar) is defined as "scaffolding." Kids will learn new information better and retain it longer if you connect the new information with something they already know and like.
- Find ways your child can learn, work, and even play in his or her area of strength. If your child's learning environment fails to capitalize on your child's strengths, make sure he or she participates in other activities that capitalize on those skills.

CONCLUSION

LouAnne abandoned a traditional school setting to open a one-room schoolhouse. Disillusioned with all forms of traditional education, she knew how many kids were getting lost in bureaucracy and mismanagement. She made it her mission to help them. The day her school opened, kids came from all over, and the one thing they had in common was consistent academic failure and a hatred of school.

With high expectations and a limited budget LouAnne prepares "her kids"—the ones everyone thinks can't learn—to go to college. She embraces a simple philosophy rooted in the belief that every child can learn, and teaches "differently-abled" students to exceed every negative evaluation ever projected about them. There are no gimmicks and no quick fixes in her classroom, just a willingness to be faithful and find what works regardless of negative projections and disabling conditions.

LouAnne makes sure no student leaves her classroom feeling like learning is impossible. Shown what their strengths are and how to use strategies to cope with their areas of weakness, kids that would have dropped out before graduation are planning for graduate school.

Some of us are going to have to abandon the traditional and the obvious to help our children. We might have to forget what is standard and try the unconventional. What needs to be remembered on this journey is that no investment of time or effort on our part is ever wasted. Some of the solutions we seek will take time and effort to find and implement. Others are right in front of us. Even when we don't know what to do, we can cling to hope and the promise our prayers will be answered.

Trust yourself as a parent. Believe your child can go far, and do whatever you have to do to help him or her get there. One day your child will achieve what no one thought possible. When this happens, you won't be surprised because you saw what your child could be all along.

Glossary of Terms

Attention Deficit/Hyperactivity Disorder. Individuals with this disability exhibit inattentiveness, impulsivity, hyperactivity, or a combination of these. Persons with the hyperactive form of ADHD often display high levels of non-goals-directed activity.

Autism. A behavior disorder characterized by impairment in social communication, social interaction, and social imagination. Those with autism often have a restricted range of interests and display repetitive behavior mannerisms, along with altered reactions to the everyday environment.

Inclusion. A special education delivery model that involves serving students in the regular education environment.

Language-Based Disorder. A deficit or problem with any function of language and communication.

Learning Disability. In simple terms, the gap between IQ and achievement. A student with a learning disability typically has above-average intelligence, but his or her performance academically does not reflect his or her intellectual ability.

When a student is referred for services due to a suspected learning disability, testing is done to determine IQ, and cognitive tests are done to determine ability. When there is a gap between IQ and performance on cognitive tests, a learning disability is frequently diagnosed.

Usually the diagnosis of a learning disability will be accompanied by a commentary discussing strengths and weaknesses in functioning and in some cases offering a specific name for a particular learning disability, such as dyslexia.

TYPES OF LEARNING DISABILITIES INCLUDE:

Dyslexia. A specific reading disability in which individuals find it difficult to recognize individual letters and whole words. Characterized in part by reversals of letters.

Visual-Spatial Dyslexia. Characterized by trouble recognizing letter symbols and sight words.

Auditory-Linguistic Dyslexia. Characterized by difficulty sounding out words that are not known. Individuals with this disability often have unusual spelling and misreading errors that are not phonetic.

Dysgraphia. A learning disability characterized by the inability to sequence words, use proper punctuation and grammar, and express thoughts in writing.

Dysphasia. A learning disability characterized by the inability to process spoken language. It may include the inability to express thoughts verbally. In other words, a child doesn't follow directions, doesn't remember what was said, and struggles to tell you what he or she needs, wants, or means.

Sequential and Spatial Dyscalculia. A learning disability affecting memory, spatial orientation, visualization, and attention to details or symbols. In other words, a child can't remember where he is or where he is going, and can't recall how to read a sign or symbol on the way—but will run all the way there.

Articulographic Dyspraxia. A learning disability affecting the ability to read orally.

Vestibulo Cerebellar Dysmetria. Refers to eye movements that cause words to blur and a child to lose his place in paragraphs and omit words.

Mainstreaming. A special education delivery model that involves serving students in a separate special education classroom and allowing students to return to regular education for subjects only when mastery has been achieved.

Obsessive-Compulsive Disorder. A psychiatric disorder; more specifically, known as an anxiety disorder. OCD is manifested in a variety of forms, but it is most commonly characterized by obsessive, distressing, intrusive thoughts, and related compulsions (tasks or rituals) that attempt to neutralize the obsessions.

Sensory Integration Deficit. The inability to filter information through the senses and use that information and respond to it.

Spectrum Disorder. The phrase "Spectrum Disorder" is often used in conjunction with issues such as Asperger's syndrome and autism. There is a continuum along which you will see varying degrees (a spectrum) of certain characteristics that are viewed as markers for disorders such as autism or Asperger's syndrome. If they are mild, these characteristics may be viewed on one end of the continuum leading to a diagnosis of Asperger's syndrome. A more intense display of the characteristics will lead to a diagnosis of autism.

Resources

Behavioral Therapy. As a part of overall treatment for ADHD and issues that have neurological and behavioral components, it is essential that individuals be taught strategies to be used in school, home, and social settings. These strategies should be used in conjunction with any other form of therapy, such as medicine.

Educational Therapy. A therapeutic approach for the treatment of learning disabilities developed by the National Institute for Learning Development (NILD), educational therapy focuses on the development of clear, efficient thinking. Students are taught strategies that enable them to overcome specific learning weaknesses.

While tutoring typically focuses on content, educational therapy builds efficient learning processes. NILD Educational Therapy teaches students *how* to think rather than *what* to think. It is skill-oriented, improving basic learning skills so students can learn, retain content, and be successful students. Students become better able to:

- stay focused on the teacher's voice
- read and understand what they have read
- accurately hear and remember what the teacher is saying
- read visual information on the board, transparencies, or computer screens
- understand the main points of what the teacher is saying and decide the significant information to record

• remember how to spell the words being recorded
• record information legibly

For more information visit www.NILD.org

Sensory Integration Therapy. Often offered by occupational therapists, Sensory Integration Therapy offers assistance to individuals who have difficulty with the way their senses receive and respond to stimuli. Therapists can teach parents how to replicate therapy strategies at home to increase the intended outcome.

Vision Therapy. Many vision problems such as eye-movement disorders, binocular dysfunctions, focusing disorders, strabismus, amblyopia, and perceptual-motor dysfunction can be significantly improved through optometric vision therapy. Vision therapy, an optometric specialty treatment, has been clinically shown to be an effective treatment for accommodative disorders (non-presbyopic eye-focusing problems), binocular dysfunction (inefficient eye teaming), ocular motility dysfunctions (eye movement disorders), strabismus (turned eye), amblyopia (lazy eye), and perceptual-motor dysfunction.

Bibliography

Attention

Armstrong, Thomas. *ADD/ADHD Alternatives in the Classroom.* VA: ASCD, 1999.

Armstrong, Thomas. *The Myth of the A.D.D. Child: 50 Ways to Improve Your Child's Behavior and Attention Span Without Drugs, Labels, or Coercion.* New York: Dutton Books, 1995.

Discipline

Dobson, James. *The New Dare to Discipline.* Carol Stream, Ill.: Tyndale House,1996.

Nelson, Jane and Lynn Lott. *Positive Discipline A-Z, Revised and Expanded 2nd Edition: From Toddlers to Teens, 1001 Solutions to Everyday Parenting Problems.* Roseville, Calif.: Prima Publishing, 1999.

Learning

Funk, David. *Teaching with Love and Logic: Taking Control of the Classroom.* Golden, Colo.: Love and Logic Press, 1995.

Schultz, Thom and Joani Schultz. *The Dirt on Learning.* Loveland, Colo.: Group, 1999.

Glenn, H. Stephen and Michael Brock. *7 Strategies for Developing Capable Students.* Rocklin, Calif.: Prima Publishing, 1998.

Learning Disabilities

Olivier, Carolyn and Rosemary Bowler. *Learning to Learn.* New York: Fireside, 1996.

Smith, Sally L. *No Easy Answers: The Learning Disabled Child at Home and at School.* New York: Bantam Books, 1995.

Smith, Sally L. *Succeeding Against the Odds: How the Learning Disabled Can Realize Their Promise.* New York: Jeremy P. Tarcher, 1993.

Strichart, Steven S. and Charles T. Mangrum. *Teaching Learning Strategies and Study Skills to Students with Learning Disabilities, Attention Deficit Disorders, or Special Needs.* New York: Allyn & Bacon, Third Edition, 2001.

Learning and Thinking Styles

Armstrong, Thomas. *In Their Own Way: Discovering and Encouraging Your Child's Multiple Intelligences.* New York: Jeremy P. Tarcher, Revised and updated, 2000.

Tobias, Cynthia Ulrich. *The Way They Learn: How to Discover and Teach to Your Child's Strengths.* Colorado Springs, Colo.: Focus on the Family, 1994.

Tobias, Cynthia Ulrich. *Every Child Can Succeed: Making the Most of Your Child's Learning Style.* Colorado Springs, Colo.: Focus on the Family, 1995.

Motivation

Smith-Rex, Susan J. *101 Creative Strategies for Reaching Unmotivated Student Learners.* Chapin, S.C.: Youth Light, Inc., 2005.

Special Education

Wilmshurst, Linda and Alan W. Brue. *A Parent's Guide to Special Education: Insider Advice on How to Navigate the System and Help Your Child Succeed.* New York: Amacom, 2005.

Temperament

Keirsey, David and Marilyn Bates. *Please Understand Me: Character and Temperament Types.* Del Mar, Calif.: Prometheus Nemesis, 1978.

Tobias, Cynthia Ulrich. *You Can't Make Me (but I Can Be Persuaded): Strategies for Bringing out the Best in Your Strong-Willed Child.* Colorado Springs, Colo.: WaterBrook Press, 1999.

Gender Differences

Gurian, Michael, et al. *Boys and Girls Learn Differently!: A Guide for Teachers and Parents.* San Francisco: Jossey-Bass, 2000.

FOCUS ON THE FAMILY®

Welcome to the family!

Whether you purchased this book, borrowed it, or received it as a gift, we're glad you're reading it. It's just one of the many helpful, encouraging, and biblically based resources produced by Focus on the Family for people in all stages of life.

Focus began in 1977 with the vision of one man, Dr. James Dobson, a licensed psychologist and author of numerous best-selling books on marriage, parenting, and family. Alarmed by the societal, political, and economic pressures that were threatening the existence of the American family, Dr. Dobson founded Focus on the Family with one employee and a once-a-week radio broadcast aired on 36 stations.

Now an international organization reaching millions of people daily, Focus on the Family is dedicated to preserving values and strengthening and encouraging families through the life-changing message of Jesus Christ.

Focus on the Family Magazines

These faith-building, character-developing publications address the interests, issues, concerns, and challenges faced by every member of your family from preschool through the senior years.

| Focus on the Family **Citizen®** U.S. news issues | Focus on the Family **Clubhouse Jr.™** Ages 4 to 8 | Focus on the Family **Clubhouse™** Ages 8 to 12 | **Breakaway®** Teen guys | **Brio®** Teen girls 12 to 16 | **Brio & Beyond®** Teen girls 16 to 19 | **Plugged In®** Reviews movies, music, TV |

FOR MORE INFORMATION

 Online:
Log on to www.family.org
In Canada, log on to www.focusonthefamily.ca

Phone:
Call toll free: (800) A-FAMILY (232-6459)
In Canada, call toll free: (800) 661-9800

More Great Resources
from Focus on the Family®

Light from Lucas
by Bob Vander Plaats
The third of four children, Lucas was severely disabled at birth. Through the silent instruction of Lucas, the author and his family relates dozens of lessons they've learned—from knowing God and discovering the value of every life, to practical ideas on parenting and why we suffer.

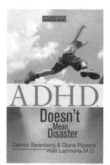

Why ADHD Doesn't Mean Disaster
by Dennis Swanberg, Dr. Walt Larimore & Diane Passno
Why ADHD Doesn't Mean Disaster provides a realistic, encouraging perspective from parents who have raised children with ADHD, as well as some who have ADHD themselves. Filled with insights, personal stories and sound medical expertise, this book gives parents facing the challenges of handling ADHD hope that breaks through the hype.

Delight in Your Child's Design
By Laurie Winslow Sargent
Every child is special, but even good parents can become discouraged by frustrating aspects in their child's makeup and personality. *Delight in Your Child's Design* will enrich the parent/child relationship by helping parents understand and appreciate the unique design, temperament, and abilities of each of their children.

FOR MORE INFORMATION

Online:
Log on to www.family.org
In Canada, log on to www.focusonthefamily.ca.

Phone:
Call toll free: (800) A-FAMILY
In Canada, call toll

BP06XP1